I0441627

Carol Baxter thought she was simply a genealogist who enjoyed writing up her research – until she discovered the story of an intriguing sex-scandal, decided to try writing the story for the commercial market, and had her first 'popular history' picked up by the first publisher she approached only two weeks after posting the manuscript. Allen & Unwin's quick response required a radical re-appraisal: she wasn't just a family historian but a writer.

In the decade since, Carol has written another five mainstream books, which are internationally-acclaimed and award-winning. She also speaks about writing and researching at genealogical conferences on land and on international cruise ships. She is a Fellow of the Society of Australian Genealogists and an adjunct lecturer at the University of New England, New South Wales.

Praise for Carol Baxter's 'popular history' books:

'Totally irresistible.' (*Independent*, UK)

'As lively and readable as a crime novel.' (*The Times*, UK)

'A fascinating history, mystery and portrait of a complex, contradictory man.' (*Daily Mail*, UK)

'A fascinating reconstruction of a real historical case ... You can't beat a good courtroom scene, and the 50-page account of Tawell's trial is as good as any I've read in a crime novel.' (*Independent on Sunday*, UK)

'A deftly woven tale.' (*Maclean's Magazine*, Canada)

'A stellar job.' (*Publishers Weekly*, International)

'Fascinating.' (*Library Journal*, USA)

'As gripping and readable as any crime novel, but all factual and based on remarkable research.' (*Sydney Morning Herald*, Australia)

'Carol Baxter is doing for Australian history what our athletes are doing for sport: making it exciting, interesting and world class.' (*Good Reading*, Australia)

'Compelling.' (*Canberra Times*, Australia)

Also by Carol Baxter:

Popular history/true historical crime

An Irresistible Temptation (Allen & Unwin, 2006)

Breaking the Bank (Allen & Unwin, 2008)

Captain Thunderbolt and His Lady (Allen & Unwin, 2011)

The Peculiar Case of the Electric Constable (Oneworld, 2013)

Black Widow (Allen & Unwin, 2015)

Chubbie Miller (Allen & Unwin, 2017)

Genealogical 'how to' publications

Writing Interesting Family Histories (2009, 2010, 2016)

Help! Historical and Genealogical Truth: How do I separate fact from fiction (2014)

Help! Why can't I find my ancestor's surname? (2015)

Writing and Publishing Gripping Family Histories (2016)

Genealogical Guides

Guide to Convict Transportation Lists (Unlock the Past, 2015): Part 1: 1788-1800 & Part 2: 1801-1812

Edited publications

General Musters of NSW, Norfolk Island & Van Diemen's Land 1811 (ABGR, 1987)

General Muster of NSW 1814 (ABGR, 1987)

Musters and Lists: NSW & Norfolk Island 1800-1802 (ABGR, 1988)

Musters of NSW & Norfolk Island 1805-1806 (ABGR, 1989)

General Muster and Land & Stock Muster of NSW 1822 (ABGR, 1989)

General Muster List of NSW 1823, 1824, 1825 (ABGR, 1999)

Convicts to NSW 1788-1812 (SAG, 2002, CD-ROM)

Writing
INTERESTING
Family Histories

Carol Baxter
The History Detective

First edition 2009
Second edition 2010
Third edition 2016
Copyright © Carol Baxter 2016

All rights reserved. No part of this book may be reproduced or transmitted in any form or by any means, electronic or mechanical, including photocopying, recording or by any information storage and retrieval system, without prior permission in writing from the publisher. The *Australian Copyright Act 1968* (the Act) allows a maximum of one chapter or 10 per cent of this book, whichever is the greater, to be photocopied by any educational institution for its educational purposes provided that the educational institution (or body that administers it) has given a remuneration notice to Copyright Agency Limited (CAL) under the Act.

Carol Baxter
The History Detective
10 Melaleuca Dr, St Ives NSW 2075, AUSTRALIA
Email: c_baxter@optusnet.com.au
Web: www.carolbaxter.com

Baxter, Carol.
Writing Interesting Family Histories.

ISBN 978-1535393454

1. Genealogy – Authorship. 2. Genealogy – Handbooks, manuals, etc. I. Title.

929.1

Printed and bound by Charles Sturt University, Bathurst.
Cover design by Alerrandre of fiverr.com.

Contents

Author's Note.. 7
Introduction... 9
Chapter:
   1. Imagination?... 12
   2. What are facts?... 14
   3. Historical 'facts'... 20
   4. Perspective 25
   5. Style, tone and voice 29
   6. Structuring a simple family history...................... 35
   7. A 'pole' structure example 40
   8. Surnames... 47
   9. Beginning a family history 51
   10. Words on the page 58
   11. Words of wisdom.. 67
   12. From dry to interesting 70
   13. The dramatic experience................................... 78
   14. Scenic experiences 88
   15. Epigraphs 98
   16. Words, words, words 105
   17. Delight in the unexpected 113
   18. The truth, the whole truth ... .117
   19. Publish or perish?.. 121
Conclusion 122
Reading List... 125
Index 126

If one could make alive again for other people some cobwebbed skein of old dead intrigues and breathe breath and character into dead names and stiff portraits. That is history to me!

George Macaulay Trevelyan

Author's Note

My interest in historical research began while I was at high school, when we studied Josephine Tey's *The Daughter of Time*, a novel telling the story of Richard III and the death of the young princes in the Tower. It was the era of Erich von Daniken's *Chariots of the Gods* and books about the mysteries of the Bermuda Triangle and both the stories themselves and the research process intrigued me. But what did a teenager with an interest in research actually research? I started tracing my family history.

As a relative was tracing my father's family, I began with my mother's. Her grandparents, parents, uncles and aunts were all dead; however, as beginner genealogy books said to interview family members, I attempted to interview a couple of her parents' cousins. I was only 18, they were 'old', I had never met them before and they weren't interested. Not enjoyable. I dumped the interview from my genealogical tool-kit.

I soon realised that I had little interest in researching recent people, anyway, that it was the long-dead, long-forgotten ones that challenged me the most. I also realised that writing up the results of my research – writing family histories – gave me as much pleasure as the research itself. Putting pen to paper not only helped the analytical process, it provided an opportunity to explore the background history and to discover information that would add colour to the narrative. As I moved from writing family histories to writing 'popular history', I faced an even greater challenge in turning dry facts and background history into interesting or even exciting narrative. It's the same challenge all family historians face.

Most examples of interesting writing in 'writing your family history' books use information extracted from anecdotes, letters, diaries and/or photographs. But what if we have none of these sources? What if our ancestors were not hoarders or if we are writing about those who lived too long ago? Let's face it, anecdotal information – letters, diaries and photographs – generally only survive for those born within the last century or two whereas most genealogists can trace their ancestry back two to five centuries, sometimes a millennium. The biggest challenge lies in bringing to life those who today are nothing more than a fading ink mark on a yellowing page.

In the following chapters, I will communicate how I bring these people and their stories to life in my popular histories and show you how to do the same in your own family histories. Most of the writing examples are drawn from my own writing because there are no copyright issues, they are easy to find, and I know what I first wrote and what I was trying to achieve.

This book was first written in 2009 and updated in 2010 at which time I had two mainstream books published. With six now under my belt, I have more information and suggestions to communicate so I decided to write a companion volume, *Writing and Publishing Gripping Family Histories*.

I have also updated this volume of *Writing Interesting Family Histories* by republishing it with a new cover, adding section headings within the chapters, adding some more explanations and examples, and generating an index.

Acknowledgements

My heartfelt thanks to my mentor and one-time boss, Keith Johnson AM, and to my friends, Kate Wingrove and Michael Flynn, for reading the manuscript and offering their suggestions. Also to Stephen Ehat for his usual excellent editing and proofreading efforts. And as always, to my supportive family who live and breathe whatever I am writing – whether they want to or not. You're all worth your weight in gold.

Introduction

Imagine that a window in time opens and we come face-to-face with an ancestor we've been researching for many years. We gaze at her in wonder for a moment then proudly tell her that we've written her life story. Pulling out a sheaf of papers, we begin reading:

> Sarah Adams was born in Deal, Kent, on 1 February 1799 to John Adams, a blacksmith, and his wife Mary, nee Jones. She was baptised on 24 March 1799 at St Mary's Church of England, Deal. On 29 July 1815 she married agricultural labourer, James Richards, by banns at St Mary's, Deal, the banns having been called on the three previous Sundays. The couple initially settled on a farm near Deal and had a daughter Margaret born there on 12 May 1816 and baptised on 28 May 1816. By 1 January 1819, when their son John was born, they had moved to London. John was baptised on 16 January 1819 at St Martin-in-the-Fields, London.
>
> On 1 March 1820 Sarah was caught stealing a length of silk fabric worth £2.4s.6d. from the shop of Mrs Ann Hardwick in London. She was taken to Newgate Gaol where she remained for six weeks before being brought to trial at the Old Bailey on 15 April 1820. She was found guilty. After another ten days in Newgate, she was returned to the Old Bailey on 25 April for sentencing. The judge ordered that she be transported to New South Wales for seven years. On 10 May 1820, Sarah was taken to the convict transport *Morley*, which was lying at Woolwich, on the Thames River. It sailed on 22 May, reaching Sydney on 30 September 1820 ...'

Glancing up at our companion, we notice an odd look on her face. For a moment there is silence, then she begins talking:

I was born during the troubles with France and for most of my childhood we lived with the fear of a French invasion. The Napoleonic Wars ended around the time I was married and I'll always remember the cheering and hooting and guns firing in the streets after Wellington won the Battle of Waterloo.

Our own troubles began not long after when my husband hurt his back. He had trouble working, then the harvests failed and he lost his job. Soon there was no other work around. Times were tough for everyone, so we moved to London to find work, but there was little around and eventually we ran out of money.

One day, when I was in a shop, I realised that everyone's attention was on someone else so I reached out and grabbed some food and hurried away. No one followed me. I began shaking with the shock of what I'd done but at least we would eat for a couple of days. I began to shoplift more and more, always fearful but with little choice, stealing anything I could grab. I'd found a fence by then, someone who would give me money for whatever I'd stolen. Not much but it helped. Then one day a man grabbed me as I slipped through the shop door and demanded that I open my jacket.

I was taken to Newgate and down the dark corridors. Hands reached through the iron bars to claw at me and voices jeered. I was thrown into a small cell with lots of other women – too many women. There was barely room to lie down. The stench from the buckets in the corner made me feel ill. Huge rats nibbled at me when I slept. And there was nothing to do, for day after day after endless day. All I could think about was being sent to the gallows and what would happen to my babies when I was gone.

The judge barely looked at me during the trial. I tried to explain my troubles but no one was interested. The jury called out guilty and the judge thumped his gavel and I was taken back to Newgate.

The following ten days were the worst. Death or life? It lay in the judge's hands. When the guards collected us and shackled us and marched us back to the Old Bailey, they mocked us. They said that we were walking along Dead Man's Walk and that the gallows' victims were buried under our feet and that some of us would soon join them. When the judge said I was to be sent to New South Wales for seven years I was so relieved. Seven years wasn't that long. But then I heard that few convicts came back home, that the government was happy to get rid of us but wouldn't pay for our return. I would be leaving my babies forever.

The trip to New South Wales was dreadful. I had never been on a ship before and the storms were terrifying, the wind squealing as if from hell itself, the ship rolling wildly. Water seeped into our quarters and started to rise and rise because the pumps weren't working properly. I thought we were going to drown. Sometimes it was so hot I thought we'd suffocate, other times so cold we huddled together for warmth. The prison fever came with us and many women got sick and a few died. I woke up one morning and the woman next to me was dead. When we reached Sydney and I was helped ashore, I couldn't stand straight and I staggered around as if I was drunk. But I was alive. Alive!'

She pauses for a moment and begins to slowly shake her head. Then she says, 'And all you could write about was the dates!'

We stammer in response that we couldn't find any other information, that the records didn't include her personal experiences.

She looks back, almost contemptuously, and asks, 'Well, why didn't you use your imagination?'

1

Imagination?

Imagination? No! No! We can't use our imagination when writing family histories. We can't make things up. We have to stick to the facts. Isn't that right?

Not quite. Using our imagination doesn't mean making things up. It means thinking outside the square. We might not find the records that allow us to hear Sarah Adams' voice, that recount her personal experiences. Yet by stepping into her shoes and empathising with her, by asking why she might have done what she did and how she must have felt, then by looking for confirmatory sources, we can get very close.

General history books cover Sarah's times, that is, the Napoleonic Wars and the ensuing economic depression as well as the rise in crime as the unemployed resorted to whatever means necessary to survive. Books about Newgate and the Old Bailey communicate their horrors in vivid detail. Journals of convicts and other travellers talk about the convict ships and the experiences of a lengthy sea voyage. Local history publications give a sense of the developing community in Australia. There is no reason to focus almost solely upon dates and other known 'facts' when writing our family histories.

Indeed, focusing solely upon these facts doesn't do justice to those we are researching. Think about Sarah Adams' recollections. Not a single date. When we recount own life story, do we simply recite dates? No. In fact, most of us struggle to remember them: the date we started school, the date we won a prize, the date we graduated, the date we began our first 'proper' job. What we remember are the experiences and how we felt – as Sarah did.

And these are much more interesting for our readers than just the dry dates.

So how do we write family histories that do not merely recount the facts but can relate what an individual must have experienced, even though we know very little about them? How can we write a family history that tells an interesting story, one that members of our families will genuinely want to read? Answering these and related questions is what this book is about.

The basics

The facts provide the skeleton of a family history and are, of course, essential. Research exhaustively. Make sure that we find every arm and leg, every finger and toe. Most family histories reveal glaring research deficiencies.

The flesh is equally as important, holding the skeleton together as well as adding individuality. We flesh out a person's life story by exploring the backdrop. Then we begin writing, using a pinch of logic and a dash of imagination to fill in the gaps.

Before we reach the chapters that discuss writing skills, we need to understand the truth about the facts that genealogists generally fixate upon when writing family histories. Understanding what dates truly are, for example, helps loosen our grip on the usual fact-focused descriptions and gives us permission to release our creative writing spirit.

2

What are facts?

Facts are facts, you are probably thinking. Surely we don't need a whole chapter to define them. The world is not flat but spherical. One plus one equals two. Night follows day. Facts.

But are facts as factual as we believe them to be? Take dates for example, the foundation stones of most family histories. Are dates facts? Are dates certainties?

The Julian-Gregorian calendar changeover

It's late one Wednesday evening and a woman is in labour with twins. With a final heave, she gives birth to the first baby. Her husband is outside the room pacing the floor. Hearing the babe's bellows of annoyance and a shout from the midwife, he looks at his grandfather clock and opens the family bible. Having already prepared the page by jotting down the year and both parents' names, he adds the final details: a daughter born at 11.55 pm on Wednesday, September 2nd. Ten minutes later another cry rings out. The husband adds another notation: a son born at 12.05 am on Thursday, September 14th.

The 14th? How could Wednesday September 2nd be followed by Thursday, September 14th? That's absurd.

But it actually happened. In September 1752 England changed from the Julian to the Gregorian calendar, falling in line with most of its European neighbours. Caesar's Julian calendar came into use in 45 BCE (Before Common Era) and proved surprisingly accurate, diverging from the solar calendar by only eleven minutes per year. That minor difference, however, had grown to eight days by 1582 CE (Common Era), when Pope Gregory XIII decreed that a new calendar was to be used. What became known as the 'Gregorian calendar' had slightly different rules for leap years to keep the civil and solar calendars in line.

Only four countries followed his decree at that time although others gradually saw the merits of the new calendar. By 1752 the Julian and Gregorian calendars diverged by eleven days – hence the gap between 2 and 14 September when England made the changeover. Russia didn't adopt the Gregorian calendar until 1918 and some minor African nations still haven't adopted it.

Thus, throughout these centuries, the dates recorded for many historical events differed depending upon whichever calendar was in use in the country at that time. Consequently, some historians use a dual dating system for the period between 1582 and 1923 (when the last European country changed its calendar) to account for the variation: for example, 3/14 September 1752. Otherwise, imagine the confusion for anyone reading English and French versions of the same military battle, one an ancestor might have fought in.

Clearly dates – the foundation stones of most family histories – are not facts in the same way that 'one plus one equals two' or 'night follows day'. Instead they are relativities, a function of whichever calendar is chosen. Some cultures have different calendars: the Jewish and Muslim cultures, for example. Is one calendar more 'correct' than any other? No, of course not. It is merely cultural usage that dictates our sense of 'correctness'.

Calendar changeover impacts

OK, you say. The calendar changeover created problems in England in September 1752 and in other places at other times but otherwise we don't need to worry about it. So what does this have to do with writing interesting family histories?

Let's think about it a bit further. We are no longer writing bland factual accounts. We are trying to think outside the square, to use our imaginations. Remember the fuss about carpets fading when day-light saving was introduced? Well, imagine the fuss when some members of the population learnt they were losing eleven days from their calendar, eleven days, they believed, from their lives! And imagine the outcry when they realised they would have to pay the same rental dues for the quarter even though there were eleven fewer days in their rental period.

Imagine if such a calendar changeover happened now. What date would we celebrate our birthday? The date it always was? But that date would no longer reflect how many days we had been alive. The new date? But that's not our 'birth-day'. Some people alive today, or recently deceased, had to make such a decision, including those born prior to 1918 in Russia and Russian-controlled territories.

Just out of interest, calculate how many ancestors would have been affected by the changeover. For someone born in the year 2000, approximately 1500 of their great-great-great-...-grandparents would have been alive in the mid-1700s. Fortunately they weren't living in a bureaucratic society, thereby lessening the day-to-day impact.

This changeover needs to be taken into consideration when researching these people. Perhaps it also rates a mention in our family histories as a curious event that happened in their lives. At the very least, writers must be cautious about saying that, for a person whose life straddled the changeover period, they were so many years/months/days old when they died.

What if a family member who reads our book is keen to explore the characters of their ancestors through the use of astrological charts? The results could offer interesting insights; however, if the researcher was unaware of this calendar changeover, it would distort the output.

Lady Day

Is the calendar issue now dealt with? Incredibly enough, no. Another changeover occurred in England in 1752, one that has particular significance for genealogists.

Prior to 1752, the first day of each year was 25 March, not 1

January. 'Lady Day', as it was known, celebrated the Feast of the Annunciation of the Blessed Virgin – that is, Jesus Christ's 'conception' nine months before his 'birth' on 25 December. Lady Day became the first day of both the calendar year and the financial year.

Thus, six months before the Gregorian calendar changeover, the date 24 March 1751 was followed by 25 March 1752. After the calendar changeover in September 1752, the New Year began on 1 January 1753. Technically, there was no 1 January to 24 March 1752.

Or was there?

Lady Day impacts

Imagine that the twins mentioned earlier were born seven months earlier on 20 February to a Scottish father and an English mother living in England. What year of birth would the father write in his family bible?

Why is this an issue? Because the Scottish changed their New Year's Day to 1 January in the year 1600. And the Holy Roman Empire in 1544, and the French in 1564, and the Russians in 1700 ...

This family bible is an original record yet we have no way of knowing what year the father was referring to without finding a confirmatory source, such as a baptism entry, or some other means of determining context, such as a reference to an earlier or later child. If the couple had no other children and if they attended a non-conformist church whose registers have not survived (the norm for non-conformist churches for the period), then simply writing that date in our family history could be misleading.

To account for this New Year discrepancy, any year involving the dates 1 January to 24 March in the pre-1752 period should be written in family records and family histories as a dual year (eg. 1751/52) – in the case of English families living in England, at least. If we are examining a source that fails to use this dual year, we must determine the guidelines used in documenting the dates.

For instance, an 'official' transcription of an English baptism or marriage entry in the *International Genealogical Index* (IGI) is likely to list the date '20 February 1751' for this child's birth – as recorded in the church register – whereas a contributor-submitted entry referring to the same event would usually record the date as '20 February 1752'. Unless we know how to distinguish between these two sources (the first character of the batch number), we could easily make an incorrect assumption. The 'fact' in our family history becomes an error.

Obviously the IGI is only a transcribed index so researchers should always check the original source. However, even after checking the original, researchers who are unaware of these date issues might not realise they are making an error.

Those in the know should always write '20 February 1751/52' to prevent such confusion. Painstaking historians write a dual-date/dual-year combination; for example, '20 February/3 March 1751/52'. No kidding.

Backwards calendars

Different calendars; different years; different days. Dates no longer seem to be facts embedded quite so firmly in history's concrete.

Of course, the one thing we can declare with absolute certainty is that, whatever calendar is in use, time marches inexorably forwards. The year 2000 is always followed by 2001. Yes?

Not when we are looking at dates from the distant past. We have the strange occurrence of our own calendar going backwards:

2 BCE (Before Common Era; previously 'BC')
1 BCE
1 CE (Common Era; previously 'AD')
2 CE

How can time go backwards? Naturally, those living in ancient times didn't have a calendar that went backwards. But we don't use their calendar. We have imposed our own calendar over their existence, a calendar that suits our particular purposes even though, oddly enough, it goes backwards.

Summary

Dates are not the absolutes – the set-in-stone 'facts' – that we once thought they were. They are relative to the calendar in use. They are always contextual and sometimes contradictory, if not completely confusing. Hopefully, our grip on dates as 'truths' is starting to be loosened.

3

Historical 'facts'

Having accepted that a date is merely part of a framework imposed over time, and having identified that framework, surely we can now accept a date within that framework as a fact, a certainty, the mainstay of our family histories.

Not quite.

Documenting the date

Has it ever occurred to you to wonder how an illiterate person living in a largely illiterate society knew what the date was?

We live in a bureaucratic society with calendars on our walls, mobile/cell phones in our pockets, computer screens on our desks, and newspapers sitting nearby; and yet – incredible as it may seem – we often don't know what the date is. Like our ancestors, we know what day of the week it is. Yet we still need to glance at one of our calendars to check the date. So think how much harder it must have been in the past.

When illiterate parents brought their children to be baptised and were asked the children's dates of birth, what did they say? Indeed, how could they possibly know what their children's birth-dates were? Calendars? Even if they were available to them (which they weren't), they couldn't have read them, being illiterate. Newspapers? Not until recent times.

It is likely that our ancestors recollected the day on which an event occurred by its relationship to another day or to an event that happened on a certain day. When was their child born? The Tuesday before Easter. The Thursday of market week. The cleric would check his calendar and write down the actual date.

Forgetfulness

These 'dates' would be easy enough to remember if the event had just occurred, but what if it occurred some months previously? Memories fade. When was it? the parent thinks. Was it the Tuesday before Easter or the Tuesday after?

Back to the twins born in 1752. They are sickly so their father sends for his local clergyman who arrives a short time later and baptises the infants. Then he heads home to his snug bed. On the following Sunday, when the parish clerk is tackling the paperwork, the clergyman remembers the baptisms and tells the clerk to add them to the register. When was it? the clerk asks. Hmm, the clergyman ponders. Was it the early hours of Wednesday morning or Thursday morning that he was dragged from his warm bed? Whatever, he decides, and says 'Wednesday'.

And as easily as that – a parent's forgetfulness, a cleric's belatedness – the dates we so happily extract from the records and copy into our family histories are wrong. Yet we treat these dates as if they are gospel truths, more important than anything else in writing our family histories.

Errors in original records

Errors abound in original records. As the editor of many published transcriptions, I've come across every imaginable type. Sometimes the wrong year or month or day was carried from one page to another (in each New Year, how long does it take us to automatically write the correct year?). Unless we are looking closely at the original record, we might not notice such an error.

Sometimes a baptism occurs before a birth or a burial before a death – according to the dates listed in the register at least. Were the dates accidentally switched? Sometimes context helps to determine the nature of the error, but not always.

Names can be listed wrongly as well. Indeed, it's surprising how often a daughter's name is accidentally repeated for the mother in a baptism entry or a son's name for the father, an error that becomes obvious when we attempt to determine the family groups of people with the same surname in a parish. The opposite must occur as well – that is, the mother's or father's name being accidentally listed for the child. How often is that responsible for our inability to trace an ancestor's birth, one that results in a genealogical dead end?

Our minds are so easily distracted. Perhaps a cleric's thoughts or conversation about his next sermon was responsible for a girl twin named *Elizabeth* Douglas being listed as a boy twin named *Joseph* in an 1814 baptism. Fortunately, later population and census returns grouped the child with her twin so the error became obvious.

Clerics sometimes jotted the details of ceremonies on scraps of paper which they handed to the parish clerk. If their handwriting was anything like their fellow professionals, the medical practitioners, it doesn't bode well for the accuracy of many registers.

Since numerous errors must have occurred in every type of record we come across, the odds are that, in the plethora of dates we proudly record in our family history, some are wrong.

And that's not simply because of the errors recorded in the original records. What about those we make ourselves when transcribing these records – initially into our notes and then later into our family histories? The general consensus is that a one-to-five percent error rate occurs in all transcriptions.

The significance of errors

Wrong information in original records? Wrong dates, in fact. This knowledge should rock the foundations of any belief that the only way to write an accurate family history is to stick to the known facts. If we can't be sure that the information in a historical record is correct – and in truth, we can't be sure about the accuracy of any historical record – then how does that affect the way in which we write our family histories?

Should we qualify everything we write? Should we write: 'John

Smith was born on 1 January 1806 – if his parents remembered the date correctly, if the local clergyman or parish clerk wrote it down correctly, if I transcribed it correctly.' But that would make any family history excruciatingly boring.

When dealing with historical facts, all we can do is assume that the information is correct. However, if we have good reason for believing otherwise, we have to weigh the evidence carefully. Many descendants of the Douglas family refused to believe that the twin *Elizabeth* was the child baptised as *Joseph*. The elaborate explanations they thought up ...

These descendants forgot one of the basic rules of detective work: Ockham's Razor. Loosely translated it says that 'of two or more explanations, the simplest is the most likely'. In the Douglas example, the simplest explanation was that the 'facts' – as listed in the church register – were wrong.

Communicating dates and other facts

Having conducted exhaustive research – and accepted the limitations of the information we have gathered – we decide that we are ready to begin writing a family history. We start putting something together but find that it reads like a series of calendar entries.

It is impossible to write an interesting family history if dates and other dry facts dominate our narrative. Think about dates. Think about the year 1759, for example. For most of us it is just a four-digit number. It means nothing.

What about 1492? Who cannot hear '1492' without feeling the urge to say, 'In fourteen-hundred-and-ninety-two, Columbus sailed the ocean blue.' And with that date comes a mental image of an old sailing ship and people dressed in old-fashioned clothes and a map of America.

What about 1788? For most family historians, that date is also meaningless. For Australians, however, it conjures up an image of eleven tall ships sailing into Sydney Harbour, of shackled convicts and red-uniformed marines and naked Aborigines standing on the shore-line watching.

What about 1945? For many, this date will generate a visceral response: memories of sadness at the death of loved ones and of happiness amidst the end-of-war celebrations.

The point being made here is that dates are only meaningful if they relate to a known historical event or a personal experience. Otherwise they are just a series of hard-to-read and easily forgettable numbers.

Summary

In these last two chapters, we have established that facts – in particular, dates – are not the set-in-stone truths we once thought them to be. In the next chapter, we explore what happens when we transform dates and other facts into prose.

5

Perspective

It is clear from the previous chapters that dates are relative to the calendar of choice and can only be considered a probability in view of the error problem. Let's now think about how we communicate dates and other facts.

Perspectives and facts

Every time we put our facts into words – that is, every time we craft prose – we communicate a perspective, unwitting though we might be. For example, an Australian family historian with First Fleet ancestry might write:

> The First Fleet sailed into Sydney Harbour in 1788.

Someone with early American ancestry might write:

> The *Mayflower* landed at Cape Cod in 1620.

Do these sentences communicate a perspective? Surely not. Both statements reflect a bald statement of facts. But what about:

> The Japanese submarines invaded Sydney Harbour in 1942.

Perspective? Absolutely, as communicated by the verb 'invaded'. Sydney Harbour was Australian territory, Australia was at war with Japan, and the Japanese had no right to enter.

Having accepted that the word 'invaded' communicates a clear perspective, let's note again the first two sentences. On their own, the words 'sailed' and 'landed' appear innocuous. Yet when juxtaposed against 'invaded', it is obvious that the words 'sailed' and 'landed' communicate a perspective as clearly as does 'invaded'.

What is that perspective? That there was nothing wrong with the First Fleet 'sailing' into Sydney Harbour or the *Mayflower* 'landing' at Cape Cod. But would the First Peoples of these two nations see it the same way? In current times, these peoples and many others describe these arrivals as territorial intrusions, as 'invasions'.

Everyone has a perspective. Think also about the convicts on board the First Fleet, who were banished from their homeland and families because they had resorted to crime to survive? Think about the sailors press-ganged into the navy while they were drunk? And the military officers who chose the tour of duty in the hope of a promotion, difficult to acquire outside war-time. And the adventure-seeking soldiers and their wives and children? How would these people have described their arrival in Australia? Each group would have had a different perspective and each perspective was not only real, it has a right to be heard.

Perspectives in action

In the past, history was written by the conquerors. We hear their voices and opinions and justifications – the party-line, so to speak. Until recently, the voices of the conquered were rarely heard. Now historians recognise the importance of allowing all voices to have their say, all perspectives to be considered.

In order to determine how perspective might distort interpretations of the past, historians need to understand what these perspectives are and how they have developed. Eurocentric arrogance underpins many early interpretations of Australian history, for example, the belief that the white conquerors with their Christian traditions were superior to the conquered blacks, and that it was the whites' 'duty' to civilise and Christianise these heathens. Similar attitudes influenced the treatment of the indigenous peoples in all of the western world's colonies.

For our purposes, let's examine family historians and their motivations to determine how these might unwittingly influence their own perspectives.

Why do we research our ancestors?

Why are we drawn to researching our family histories? Have we some deep psychological need to understand who we are, that leads us to begin researching our origins? Probably. For many, at least. Others will be curious for medical reasons or because of a distinctive familial characteristic. In my case, after reading the books mentioned in the Author's Note, my desire was to investigate something. Anything. I even thought about joining the police! (I was too small.)

Thrill of the hunt

For many of us, the simple curiosity that prompted us to begin researching our origins soon transforms into an addiction to the hunt. The 'thrill of the hunt' researchers love the research process itself. They don't care whether their ancestors were 'good' or 'bad'. Accordingly, they are more likely to adequately research their origins and to write something that accurately reflects the family's history – if they have developed enough skills as a researcher. To hunt-driven researchers, the truth matters. The truth is all.

Fame hunters

Most of us have encountered genealogists who wrap themselves in the cloak of their ancestors' fame or infamy. They are 'proud' of their descent from Royalty or Mayflower passengers or First Fleeters, so proud in fact that everyone hears about it.

Remember the old adage 'pride before fall'? It always springs to mind when I hear family historians talk about being proud of their ancestors. *Pride* denotes possession. We might say 'I am proud of my children' because we have a direct involvement in their achievements. However we wouldn't say '*I am proud* of Nicole Kidman's achievements' for the simple reason that we have no personal involvement in them. We use the word *admire* when the connection is impersonal.

In terms of our family histories: where does the 'pride' dividing line sit, the point where we move from feeling proud of our ancestors' achievements to simply admiring them (or otherwise)? We should try to determine our own perspective by asking ourselves why we are researching our ancestry, and whether the word 'pride' is part of our family history vocabulary.

Why does it matter? Because if a family historian feels too possessive about their ancestors, they risk losing their impartiality. As a case in point, how impartial are most parents?

The 'fame hunting' family historian will readily link themselves to someone 'important' and fight tooth-and-nail if anyone questions the connection. They are interested only in 'good' ancestors and 'good' information about their ancestors, and ignore anything bad. In fact, I've recently heard of a client cancelling a research contract after the researcher discovered something bad and refusing to take receipt of the information. For 'fame hunting' researchers, their ancestors can do no wrong and woe betide anyone who dares to suggest otherwise. Indeed, hell hath no fury as a family historian whose rose-coloured glasses are in danger of being knocked off.

These family historians tend to write hagiographies – that is, works of a worshipful or idealising nature – rather than biographies because they see their ancestors not only as extensions of themselves but as reflections of themselves.

We are not our ancestors

It is essential to remember that we are not our ancestors. Their 'achievements' – luck of the draw as often as not – are not our achievements. They were not perfect and nor are we.

Why is this relevant in a book about writing interesting family histories? For two reasons:

First, we must make sure that the truth – good or bad – *does* get in the way of a good story. We are not writing fiction.

Second, goody-two-shoes family histories can be like eating sugar candy: a small dose is enjoyable but too much leaves us feeling nauseous.

Writing about those who were not perfect is a lot of fun. Indeed, I have made a writing career out of doing so.

5

Style, tone and voice

Postmodernist historians argue, among other things, that there are no facts, only probabilities and perspective. As we have seen in the previous three chapters, they have a point. Some postmodernist historians therefore argue that we might as well write fiction.

Faction

Faction as a writing style is a product of this post-modernist view. Writers research the facts then add drama, dialogue and description to give the narrative more immediacy. Readers feel as if they have stepped into the story because the story reads like fiction. However, many works of faction are little more than fiction based on a true story.

If genealogists want to write their family history as faction – fact and fiction mixed – they can. There are many different ways to write family histories and no way is more 'right' than any other.

However, it isn't necessary to fictionalise family histories to make them interesting. This is shown in the following pages.

Encyclopaedic style

Many genealogists write their family histories in an encyclopaedic style because they believe that such a style allows them to communicate the facts without overlaying their own opinions or perspective. We have already seen that facts are not necessarily *facts* and that perspective oozes from everything we write. Let's now explore the other problems with the encyclopaedic style.

Why is it that we can read a 300-page novel in one sitting but feel exhausted before we've read even a few pages of an encyclopaedia? It's not the font and layout, although they can be intimidating in themselves. It's the contents. All facts.

Facts are like hammer blows pounding away at our brains. We don't notice the effects at first but before long, as fact follows fact, as date follows date, we start skimming the prose then, without necessarily having found the information we want, we gladly put the volume aside. This is the problem genealogists face when they choose an encyclopaedic style of family history writing. If dates and other facts are allowed to dominate the narrative, the resulting family history will read like a lengthy and tedious encyclopaedia entry.

Novels, by contrast, are full of sensory details that spark readers' imaginations, that bring life to a narrative, that allow readers to experience whatever the protagonist is experiencing. Readers becomes absorbed in the narrative and keep reading – even when they shouldn't.

We all want our readers to find our family histories interesting and absorbing. Yet most of us don't want to fictionalise our family histories. This means that we have to find a different writing style to communicate the results of our research in an interesting way.

Journey of discovery

If we are writing a biography of a single individual, we could write it as a journey of discovery that details our own experiences in researching the family. This technique carries the reader with us on our journey and can prove an effective way to write a short biography or to begin a family history. It is particularly effective if the family proved challenging or exciting to research.

A friend was struggling to find information about a family that left England in 1870. Unable to locate her ancestor's birth, she began looking sideways. One of her ancestor's siblings was an English clergyman. She found a short published biography of him that mentioned a book containing information about his family.

The book turned out to be a pedigree of Noble families. From my friend's seeming dead end, she found she was descended from numerous Kings of England, France, Spain, Russia ... back to the Dark Ages. All these royal ancestors for a family she couldn't trace back before the 1840s. To fail to tell the story of this discovery would be to ignore her most exciting genealogical experience.

We've all had exciting discoveries even if they aren't as momentous as finding Royal ancestry. For example, after finishing university, I bought a one-way ticket to England so I could travel and also gather information for a genealogical thesis. I had chosen a family of Scottish immigrants for the thesis but had nothing but names for their grandparents, a couple who needed to be covered in the thesis. I doubted I would find anything more.

I tracked the grandparents back to Shotts parish, Lanarkshire, where they were living on the estate of a British Army colonel in the 1790s. They had suddenly appeared in the parish, or so it seemed, because the poorly-maintained church registers didn't list any previous instances of the surname. I decided to trace the colonel to see what I could find about him and his estate. As I was doing so, it suddenly occurred to me that my ancestor might have served in the army with him. Eventually, by exhaustive research and the occasional flashes of inspiration, I developed a complex theory: that my ancestor, John Watson, had served with the colonel in the American War of Independence and had been repatriated with him (the other rank-and-file were abandoned in America), and that he had slipped away from the regiment when the colonel took half-pay and settled with him on his Scottish estate. But I had no proof.

I hitchhiked from Shotts to the church graveyard (the foolish things young genealogists do when broke and desperate to find information) but couldn't find a headstone. Eventually I discovered that, shortly before his death, he settled with his son in Edinburgh. I found his burial and then, luck of all luck, a will. It contained a reference to his military pension. This helped prove my entire convoluted theory. Instead of including only a brief paragraph about this man in the resulting family history, I ended up with an amazing story covering his involvement in the American War of Independence between 1775 and 1781, the results of which contributed to Britain's decision to colonise Australia – where his grandson settled eighty years later.

What an ideal way of bringing this family history full-circle. Purely by chance I had discovered that the story of these men reflected not only their personal histories, but world history. And therein lay the seeds of my conclusion. But I'll talk about conclusions in the Conclusion.

We should keep these types of discoveries in mind when writing our family histories. Readers like to be participants, to connect with our story. They know us, or feel they can relate to us because of our family membership, and they are happy to take vicarious pleasure in the excitement of our discoveries. This is because genealogical searches are like detective hunts. Think how popular crime television and crime novels are. It's the excitement of the hunt that addicts most of us to genealogy and we can try to communicate some of this excitement when writing our family histories.

So how could we start a journey of discovery? We could write:

> Mary Ann Chester and I had a difficult relationship for many years. She was determined to hide her roots, to thwart my efforts to trace her – or so it seemed at the time. Then I made an amazing discovery ...

Our readers are already gripped before we begin telling our tale of action, adventure, drama, mystery or whatever else we are about to communicate.

As mentioned above, this style is best suited to short biographies or to the introductory section of a family history where we discuss the problems we faced in researching our family of interest. It can also be used for family history articles. However, it cannot be used for the entire body of a multi-generational family history.

Narrative non-fiction

My mainstream writing genre is known as 'narrative non-fiction' – that is, history told as a story. My books are proof that we don't need to fictionalise history to make it interesting. In the words of a *London Times* reviewer, *The Peculiar Case of the Electric Constable* is 'as lively and readable as a crime novel'.

Clearly, fictionalisation is unnecessary. Story-telling, however, is essential. I discuss story-telling further in later chapters of this book and in *Writing and Publishing Gripping Family Histories.*

Distant voice and bland tone

In the same way that we don't need to use an encyclopaedia style, we don't need to use a bland narrative voice, which is another feature of most family histories. It has probably never occurred to most family historians that the tone of an author's writing voice is critical to a work's reception. Most family historians – and historians for that matter – stick with a distant self-effacing narrative voice, an attempt to communicate no tone at all. Unfortunately, the resulting prose is as dry as an encyclopaedia entry.

Intimate voice

Novels try to be up-close-and-personal and are written with a more intimate narrative voice. It's not hard to work out which is the easiest to read.

We could write a family history with a more intimate tone:

> As England basked in the glory of the triumph at Waterloo, Sarah completed the preparations for her marriage. For weeks, the only topic of conversation had been the nation's magnificent victory, but this was her day.

This style can be tricky to maintain. It works best if we have lots of personal information relating to our ancestor – diaries and letters, for example – the type of sources that help us gain a deeper sense of the person's character.

I discuss 'voices' further in the companion volume.

Ironic tone

An ironic tone works well if the narrative includes extremes of good or bad behaviour. This tone intimates 'aren't we wonderful (or truly dreadful) but let's not take ourselves too seriously'. Best to forget smug self-congratulation or shrieks of moral outrage. They become tedious very quickly.

Summary

Style, voice, tone: most family historians push these tools aside as they rummage through their writer's tool-box, having no comprehension of their importance. To make the best use of them, start by thinking about who we are writing for (ourselves and our immediate family or a broader family?) and what we are trying to convey.

Writing family histories can be as much fun as researching our family's history – when we know how. I am now more addicted to the writing process than the research process which, considering the fact that I have devoted my life to historical research, is really saying something.

Moreover, the writing process itself can have astonishing benefits for our research. As we put pen to paper, we sometimes discover that we haven't enough facts, enough evidence, to firmly establish a conclusion and have to seek more. Sometimes we discover new avenues to research, things we had missed, and can add them to our research task list. Occasionally, we find that the clue was there all along in our files, that we might have already collected information about our ancestor's forebears, previously thought to be unknown, but hadn't made the connection. It's happened to me and to everyone I know who has done the same.

We make these discoveries because our brains don't simply regurgitate. As we seek the words to craft sentences of prose, our brains analyse and interpret and question. So it's a good idea to make the most of this valuable analytical tool.

6

Structuring a simple family history

Have you ever attempted to count how many ancestors you have? Two parents, four grandparents, eight great-grandparents, sixteen great-great-grandparents and so on, doubling every generation back to the dawn of time.

Well, not quite. There were not billions of people living on earth in the past, so we actually have the same ancestral couples sitting on many different branches of our hoary old ancestral trees (google 'pedigree collapse' to understand more). Even though the known double-ups reduce the number of ancestors we are researching, we still have a formidable number to choose from when deciding to write a family history. Where do we begin?

In truth, the only ancestral line we can research with any certainty is our mother's-mother's-mother's-mother's ... line. A man's involvement is little more than a blink (or wink) of the eye and can only be confirmed by DNA tests or distinctive familial characteristics whereas a woman's pregnancy and the child's birth are obvious to all. However, in the same way that we have to assume that dates and other genealogical 'facts' are correct, we have to assume that paternity is correct. This is important because it is easier to focus upon surname lines when writing a family history and, in the past, surnames were generally passed on by the male members of our families.

Simple family history structures
So which families should we write about? Let's start with six simple frameworks for our family histories. I have classified these as follows:

Pole-shaped

We write about our ancestors for one surname line only for as many generations as desired. For example, we might start with a chapter about our most distant ancestor with the surname Chester then devote the second chapter to his son, the one we are descended from, then the third chapter to his grandson, and so on. We write a chapter about each of our ancestors until we reach our most recent Chester ancestor, a daughter who married, say, a Brown. Our Chester ancestral line ends with that daughter so any of her descendants are covered in a pole-shaped family history documenting the Brown family.

Alternatively, we might write a pole-shaped family history that documents our ancestor in each generation but crosses surnames lines. A family history devoted to our female ancestors – our mother and her mother and *her* mother and so on – would be a surname-crossing, pole-shaped family history.

Broom-shaped

We write about a single surname line (a pole-shape) then, from a particular couple onwards, we expand the family history to include all descendants for a certain number of generations. This style is often used for migrant families. For example, in section one of the family history we could write a chapter about each surname-line ancestor who lived in England, ending with the couple who emigrated. Section two could document the emigrant couple's first child and his or her descendants. Section three could document their second child and descendants. And so on.

It is not wise to document every descendant of a particular immigrant family, or all descendants from any family. The more people are documented, the less in-depth research is undertaken. Family histories that document every known descendant usually end up being *prose family trees* rather than family histories.

Pyramid-shaped

We pick an ancestral couple and document every descendant for a certain number of generations (or down to the present day).

I used this framework for structuring my First Fleet family history because I knew nothing about the couple's British origins. Section one included two chapters about the First Fleet couple and a chapter each about two of their children, those who had no known descendants. Section two included a chapter about the First Fleeters' son, George, and his wife and a chapter about each of their children. Section three included a chapter about the First Fleeters' daughter Sarah and her husband, John Williams, and a chapter about each of the Williams children. The detailed biographies were limited to these first three generations: 29 people in total.

The publication also provided a pocket biography (discussed later) for the fourth generation, and noted the years of birth and death only for the fifth generation. A blank chart was included at the end of the book so that descendants could list the names of each couple in each generation of their own ancestral line.

V-shaped

We write about all of our ancestral couples coming down to the present day to the one person at the base of the V: ourselves. This strategy is best followed if three or less generations are covered. For example, we write about all eight of our grandparents, all four of our grandparents, both of our parents and ourselves. It is helpful to divide our family history into sections to make it clear which horizontal (generational) or vertical (surname line) family is being discussed.

Hourglass-shaped

We write about all our ancestors for a couple of preceding generations (a V-shaped family history) and all our descendants for the next generation or two.

Dog's dinner

We write about a confusing mish-mash of ancestors, and sometimes descendants as well, with little coherent structure. I discuss this further under 'Digressions' in the companion volume.

William Nash = Maria Haynes   ≠   Robert Guy
1789 (c1771-1844)   (c1772-1820)
[Chapter 1]   [Chapter 2]

Sarah Nash
(1798-1875)
= 1814
John Williams
(c1786-1854)
[Chapter 16]

George Nash
(1797-1870)
= 1826
Mary Lees
(1809-1877)
[Chapter 5]

William Nash
(1795-1808)
[Chapter 4]

Mary Nash
(1793)
= 1810
Robert Hall
(1770-1831)
[Chapter 3]

John Nash
(c1791)

William Nash
(1788-1789)

Henry Nash
(1847-1864)

Eliza Nash
(1845-1911)
= 1868
Ezra Emanuel Turner
(1846-1905)
[Chapter 15]

Maria Nash
(1843-1885)
= 1861
Edmund Baines
(c1835-1915)
[Chapter 14]

Sarah Nash
(1840-1909)
= 1859
John Fell
(1838-1884)
[Chapter 13]

Mary Nash
(1838-1900)
= 1861
George James Newman
(1841-1927)
[Chapter 12]

James Nash
(1836-1921)
= 1860
Mary Ann Drayton
(1841-1922)
[Chapter 11]

William Nash
(1834-1899)
= 1856
Elizabeth Annesley
(c1835-1876)
[Chapter 10]

Samuel Nash
(1833-1880)
= 1864
Sarah Berry
(c1847-1926)
[Chapter 9]

Esther Nash
(1831-1874)
= 1. 1849
John Warrington
= 2. 1864
George Bailey
(c1836)
[Chapter 8]

John Nash
(1829-1892)
[Chapter 7]

George Nash
(1827-1899)
= 1854
Eliza Thomson
(1834-1908)
[Chapter 6]

William Williams
(1844-1897)
= 1871
Catherine McDonald
(1853-1919)
[Chapter 29]

Edward Williams
(1843-1900)
= 1864
Mary Ann Rawson
(1844-1927)
[Chapter 28]

George Williams
(1838-1906)
= 1862
Janet Crawford
(c1842-1927)
[Chapter 27]

David Williams
(1836-1908)
= 1858
Mary Ann Ward
(1836-1923)
[Chapter 26]

Susannah Williams
(1833-1866)
= 1. 1849
Charles Collman
(1818-1858)
= 2. 1859
William Brown
(c1836-1863)
[Chapter 25]

John Williams
(1831-1879)
= 1858
Esther Kilpatrick
(1837-1911)
[Chapter 24]

Eliza Williams
(1829-1905)
= 1849
George Day
(1826-1906)
[Chapter 23]

Maria Williams
(1827-1892)
= 1850
Thomas Gait
(1821-1896)
[Chapter 22]

Elizabeth Williams
(1824-1906)
= 1846
Amos Crisp
(1813-1881)
[Chapter 21]

Sarah Williams
(1822-1844)
= 1844
Joseph Connors
(c1810-1892)
[Chapter 20]

Ann Williams
(1820-1872)
= 1843
Martin Hyland
(1813-1865)
[Chapter 19]

Mary Williams
(1817-1901)
= 1. 1833
Thomas Brown
(c1805-1851)
= 2. 1852
Edward Carrigan
(c1818-1871)
[Chapter 18]

Robert Williams
(1815-1880)
= 1835
Susannah Tindall
(1817-1901)
[Chapter 17]

Explanatory chart

It is critical that we provide a family tree or chart at the front of our publication displaying the connections between the relevant people and the chapter in which we document that particular person or couple. For example, with the Nash family history – a pyramid-shaped family history – I included the family chart shown on the previous page. Readers can see at a glance which person/couple was documented in each chapter. Thus it provides a visually easy-to-comprehend display of the book's structure.

If our book's structure cannot be easily displayed in a chart or tree, we are either covering too many people or are producing a 'dog's dinner' style of family history.

Which structure?

Which family history structure should we choose? For a many-generational family history, one of the first three frameworks works best. The circumstances of our family-of-interest dictates which framework we should choose.

If we follow a single surname line – a pole-shaped structure – we are also following a simple chronology, which is a structure our brains can easily understand and absorb. This is the structure outlined in the next chapter and follows the KISS principle (Keep it simple, stupid!). I originally used the pole-shaped structure to write all of my family histories and called them 'formula family histories' because I used the same formula or format for each family. Having a simple format to follow makes it easy to start writing a family history. Once the words are on the page, we can then break out and be more creative.

7

A 'pole-structure' example

The following 'Chester' example is purely hypothetical, produced only for the purposes of this publication.

Title
When producing a family history using one of the first three structures mentioned in the previous chapter – pole, broom or pyramid – it is best not to make the mistake of thinking up an eloquent title that ignores the surname of the family we are writing about. Think library catalogues and search engines. Think book stock piled up in our garages because no one stumbles across the publication on the internet. For these reasons, I gave my Nash family history the following title:

Nash

First Fleeters and Founding Families
A Three-Generational Family History

Although this title is unexciting, it communicates the critical words that allow researchers and search engines to pick it up: *Nash*, *First Fleet*, *Family History*. For a family history title, it is more important that our book is easily located than that the title is poetic.

Introduction
It is essential to introduce the family we are writing about and to position them in their historical context. It is also critical that our introduction is interesting. If we stumble off the starting blocks,

the race may be over before it has even begun. Introductions are discussed further in chapter nine.

Researching the family

Somewhere in our family history, perhaps at the start, perhaps in an appendix, it is helpful if we discuss the major problems we encountered and the conclusions we reached during our research. This would be our 'Researching the Family' section and would cover us in the event that anyone questions our conclusions, particularly as we might struggle to remember our reasoning and, as a result, be left floundering. It is best if we are open about our research processes. Family historians who are reluctant to explain their reasoning are often hiding shoddy research with questionable conclusions and sometimes even a hidden agenda.

It is important that this information is NOT included in the text of our biographies. Mixing narrative and analysis within a biography can make it seem disjointed and confusing, leaving our readers feeling bogged down by the detail. Readers have a simple solution when that occurs: they skip it. Or even worse: they put the book down. So keep analysis out of our biographies.

We could perhaps use a footnote or endnote for this purpose, however the advantage of describing the full process in the Researching the Family section is that we can treat each generation consecutively. Accordingly, the reader can see how we tackled the research process and, frankly, gain a sense of our abilities as a researcher. Covering such big-picture explanations in footnotes or endnotes is piece-meal in effect.

There is no need to state the obvious. That would bore everyone. Just explain the problematic or unusual finds. In ten years' time, we are unlikely to be able to remember exactly what led us to reach our conclusions. It could prove important.

If we have written the Researching the Family section as an exciting journey of discovery, we could include it at the start of the publication. If we have taken a third-person analytical approach, it would be best to place this information in an appendix.

Family 1:
This chapter (or chapters) documents the first family covered in our family history, the first known family to carry our surname of interest; for example, Family 1: John Chester and Mary Ann Lang. This is essentially a biography covering the lives of both the husband and wife. If the wife was a well-documented person in her own right, she could be treated separately.

Pocket biographies
After we finish the biography, we provide a list of the couple's children in pocket-biography format as shown below:

> **1. Richard Chester (see Family 2)**
> Born: 29 April 1766, Ullingswick HEF ENG.
> Baptised: 14 May 1766, Ullingswick Parish HEF ENG.
> Married: **Mary Chadwick**, 14 March 1788, St John's,
>   Worcester WOR ENG.
> Died: 1 November 1820, Worcester WOR ENG.
> Buried: 2 November 1820, St Mary's Worcester, WOR ENG.
> Offspring: Margaret (1789-1790), Thomas (1791-1849),
>   Mary Catherine (1793-1820) ...

If the husband or wife married twice and had offspring to both relationships, we restructure the marriage details as shown below. We can also choose to list the number of offspring (as shown below) rather than providing names and other details. This works best if we are devoting a later chapter to the family because it represents our ancestral line.

> ...
> Married:
> 1. **Mary Chadwick**, 14 March 1788, St John's,
>   Worcester WOR ENG.
> 2. **Ann Jones**, 19 June 1792, St Mary's, Worcester
>   WOR ENG.
> Offspring: 2 + 6

If we are not writing an individual chapter about a person or couple referred to in a pocket biography, we could add lines to the pocket biography documenting other information found: occupation, residence and so on. We could even include an additional paragraph of prose that contains, say, further biographical information or a paragraph of text from a newspaper item or obituary. Don't include long screeds of unimportant information. Stick to the useful or interesting.

We should try to keep these offspring details to two or three pages so our readers can see the details for all of the couple's children at a glance. Readers often like to see how many of the couple's offspring lived to adulthood and married, and where they ended up. Sometimes, they like to quickly tot up how many grandchildren a couple had.

In a narrative family history, it is unwise to include pedigree charts that cover dozens of pages, with siblings listed many pages apart because they are separated by generations of descendants. Experienced genealogists have enough trouble trying to find all the children born to one couple when perusing these types of family histories so imagine the difficulties non-genealogists would face. The average family member will flip the pages back and forth in utter confusion and then toss the book aside.

However, these types of pedigree charts are perfect for publishing on the internet. Search engines like Google enable researchers to easily find a particular person mentioned in the chart. The researchers who link themselves to our family can then contact us so it is important that we keep our email addresses up-to-date on our website. If we have published a family history in book form, this internet exposure can also serve as a publicity vehicle to help with book sales.

In a family history covering only the ancestral surname line, one of the children listed in the pocket biographies at the end of 'Family/Chapter 1' is the next generation to be discussed in the family history. Against that child's details, we add 'See Family 2' or 'See Chapter 2'.

Family 2

This is a new chapter or section that covers the lives of the husband and wife in the second generation of the family of interest; that is, Richard Chester and Mary Chadwick, as shown previously.

... And so on down to ...

Family ?

This is the final family carrying the surname of interest. Most ancestral surname lines end when our female ancestor married a man with a different surname. The ancestral line is then carried on under the husband's surname. So there are two possibilities for this final family. We could end with her parents' biography and, if desired, include more detailed information in her own pocket biography (and perhaps direct the reader to a published or intended-to-be-published family history that includes her story). Alternatively, we could include a full biography for the woman and her husband.

Conclusion

Any story should have a beginning, middle and end. While a conclusion is optional in a family history of the pole-shaped structure, it is advisable as it neatly rounds up the family history. It is essential in a theme-based family history. See this publication's conclusion for further information about conclusions.

Reference Notes/Endnotes

It is critical that we source-reference the material used in our family histories. The details from original records like church, census and land records are included in the Reference Notes, which are otherwise known as (and hereafter called) the Endnotes. Some authors, generally academics, include sources as Footnotes at the bottom of a page. While the choice is ours, source references at the bottom of a page suggest a heavy academic tome rather than an interesting family history. For further information see chapter ten.

Bibliography
This should include the secondary-source publications – otherwise known as authored works – used in our family histories; that is, the books, journals and websites that provide general background information or, sometimes, specific information relating to our ancestors. For further information see chapter ten.

Index
All published family histories must have an index. Collateral connections will rarely want to read the entire book to find information. Some closer family members won't want to either – sadly.

Many computer programs can help with indexing, although names can be problematic (a name can appear as, say, 'John Smith' in the text but needs to appear as 'Smith, John' in the index). If we plan to generate an index manually for that reason, it is best to leave the indexing process until the pages are typeset then leave them alone. The slightest change (even one character) can send a line over to the next page and mess up the indexing thereafter.

Some family histories contain multiple indexes, with people's names and place names in their own sections. Others group names, places and ships in special sections within a single index. If these sorts of divisions are made, we should make sure that EVERY column begins with the full section details so our readers can make sense of the index. For example, if we group place-names together, it is best to indent the different levels and to show all the relevant levels at the top of each column. This is shown below:

```
Places:
  England:
    Surrey:
      Camberwell  ...
      Epsom       ...
      Guildford   ...
```

Summary

If we choose one of these simple family history structures, it is critical that we direct the reader to the 'next' chapter by including 'See Family ...' or 'See Chapter ...' against the details for the relevant child in his or her pocket biography.

It is also helpful if we use clear section breaks where relevant – based on regions, a new surname line, and so on. Family histories can be confusing to the uninitiated. If we are self-publishing a family history, most of our sales will be to family members who are not genealogists. Making it easy for our readers is critical.

We don't need to determine how we will divide up a family history when we start writing. These types of divisions can be made after we have finished the first draft, indeed at any time until the index is produced. The wonders of computers. How did we ever write without them?

8

Surnames

I was recently talking to a group of family historians and asked how many had researched the origins and meaning of every ancestral surname they were tracing. No one had – except me.

Surnames are fascinating, shedding light on the origins of our families hundreds of years ago. Most of us will never be able to trace our families back to the surname period, to the time when 'bynames' (eg. John the carpenter) became hereditary 'surnames' (eg. John Carpenter). Yet the origin of a surname is a logical place to start a family history, particularly one that traces a single surname line.

Essentially, there are four types of surnames, as discussed below. It is helpful to know what they are as this can influence the way in which we begin our family history.

Locational surnames
Surnames deriving from locational names can be generic, some obviously so: *Hill*, *Street*, *River*, *Field*. The less obvious include my husband's surname *Ashmore* which means 'dweller at the ash trees by the lake'.

Some locational surnames derive from the name of a single place. For example, the surname *Broxholm* 'island in a brook' comes from a place-name in Lincolnshire. Many landed families in the post-Norman Conquest period became known by the name of their estate. These bynames became hereditary surnames in the 1100s or 1200s – in England at least – which was much earlier than the masses acquired surnames. Hereditary surnames, like most fashions, began with the upper classes. This social group needed to prove their title to land and other assets and could only do so by distinguishing themselves from others with the same popular given name. The acquisition of surnames drifted down through society's layers over the following few hundred years.

Some researchers who carry or descend from a 'gentry' surname proudly announce their descent from the gentry itself. Upon questioning, however, they will often admit to a gap of a couple of hundred years between the pedigrees delineated in the Heralds' *Visitations* of the 1500s and 1600s and their own family. Similarly to many other family historians, they have been unable to trace their own line back before the 1700s or early 1800s.

To claim certain descent from such a family when documenting the origins of a surname is not recommended. As starters, to assume there is a gap of only a couple of hundred years is problematic in itself as we might descend from a younger son who made his own way in the world hundreds of years earlier, perhaps even before the family acquired their status or wealth. Or we might descend from someone who worked on the estate or who left the estate around the surname period. John Chester's ancestors, for example, almost certainly didn't own the town of Chester. The family probably acquired the byname *Chester* because their progenitor once lived there but had left the place; that is, he became known as, say, *William of Chester* to distinguish him from the other Williams in his new neighbourhood. *Chester* became a hereditary surname in his children's generation.

It is also important to recognise that a surname might have been assumed at some point in the twenty to thirty generations since the surname period, perhaps because a child took the name of a step-father or because a nefarious ancestor required an alias.

And, of course, the ancestor responsible for our surname of interest might have been a woman.

Occupational surnames

My own surname, *Baxter*, is an occupational surname deriving from 'baker' – but not, usually, a male baker. In the same way that *spinster* derived from 'female spinner', *Baxter* derived from 'female baker'. Having a female surname does not necessarily suggest illegitimacy. Widows also had to support themselves and their families.

Smith, the most common English surname, reflects the prevalence of this occupation in the Middle Ages (and the fertility of its carriers). Many occupational surnames are obvious and readily identifiable – *Taylor, Cook, Butler* – although it is wise to confirm the origin, just in case. Many others are unrecognisable for a variety of reasons. The occupation itself might no longer exist (eg. *Deathridge*, a tinder-maker). The occupational term might no longer be used (eg. *Lister*, a dyer). The occupational term might have been shortened (eg. *Garlick*, from garleker or garlekmonger, a seller of garlic).

Some apparent occupational names might have once been nicknames; for example, *Abbot(t)* and *Monk*, because members of the clergy in the surname period were supposed to be celibate. However, the church estates were large employers in the surname period and such surnames may simply indicate that the progenitor of the family worked for the abbot or monk.

Personal names

Jones, the second commonest English surname, derives from the personal name *John* as do many other surnames. Sometimes the origin is obvious: *Rogers, Rogerson*. Note: the '-s' ending occurs more often in the south of England and the '-son' ending in the north and Scotland. Note also that the '-s' ending might reflect a possessive: 'Roger's servant' rather than 'Roger's son'.

Sometimes the origin isn't obvious: *Symes* or *Simpkinson*, '(son of) Simon' through its diminutive *Sims* or double diminutive *Simkin*. Often the origin is completely obscured: *Hotchkiss* from *Roger* through its diminutive *Hodge*.

A relationship can be reflected in a prefix as well as a suffix. The Scottish *Mac-* and Welsh *ap* signify 'son of', while the Irish *O'* signifies 'grandson/descendant of'. The Welsh *ap* is no longer seen on its own but has often inserted itself at the start of a name: *Bowen* derives from 'ap Owen' and *Pugh* from 'ap Hugh'. Hereditary surnames developed much later in Wales than in England, beginning to become hereditary among the gentry in the 1400s.

Some surnames derive from women's personal names. My mother's maiden name *Christie* is from *Christian*, which was more often a female given name in Scotland in the Middle Ages. *Magg* and *Pogge* are from *Margaret*, *Molle* from *Mary*. Some surnames derive from Anglo-Saxon personal names (*Goodwin*) and Viking names (*Osgood*). The Norman Conquest was responsible for most of the well-known English personal names, including *Richard*, *Robert*, *Roger* and *William*, and their associated surnames.

Nicknames

Nicknames include simple colour names (*Brown*, *Redhead*), physical characteristics (*Cruikshank* 'bowlegged' or *Vidler* 'wolf-face'), mental and moral characteristics (*Sharp*, *Wise* or *Gutsell* 'good soul'), animal, bird and plant names (*Colt* or *Pinnell* 'upright as a young pine') and derogatory or jocular phrases (*Godsave*, *Drinkale* and *Scattergood* 'spendthrift'). Indeed, every nickname applied to humans in the surname period was no doubt responsible for at least one surname.

Summary

Despite the centuries that lie between a surname's acquisition and the present day, surnames can still communicate the essence of a person.

Australia once had men with the surnames *Hawke* and *Peacock* as federal political leaders at the same time, one leading the government, one the opposition. When Australians picture these two men, it seems obvious why their ancestors acquired such surnames. Isn't it astonishing that hundreds of years later these men could still reflect their ancestors' distinctive characteristics?

Or perhaps they grew to be like their surnames.

9

Beginning a family history

There are so many different ways to start a family history that they cannot all be communicated. But here are some ideas to get started.

Introductions

For a locational surname relating to a placename, the simplest way to start a family history is by discussing the place.

Introduction

The roots of the Chester family probably lie in the English town of Chester, which sits on the River Dee a short distance from the Welsh border.

OK. OK. I know this is dry – to say the least – and these are just the facts but this is a really easy way to get started. Remember: words on the page.

Words on the page

Any writing starts with getting words on the page. Anyone who thinks that famous authors write beautiful prose as soon as they put pen to paper or fingers to keyboards should think again. Some of the greatest novels have taken many years to write. Considering that authors can write 1000-3000 words a day and that the average novel is 100,000 words (that is, one to three months of writing time), they have clearly spent a considerable amount of time shaping their stories and polishing their prose.

It always seems bizarre that schools and universities assess students' knowledge based on first-draft essays written under exam conditions. No publisher would publish a first draft of any piece of prose.

Adding life to our introduction

What brings our writing to life, what makes history vivid and readable, are the sensory details mentioned earlier. So how do we find the type of sensory details that will bring our introduction to the Chester family history to life?

Let's start by looking into Chester's history. A google search reveals that Chester began its life as a Roman fort, and that later Anglo-Saxon settlers continued to call it *Legacæstir*, meaning 'fortress-city of the legions'. The retention of the last part of the Latin name evolved to become 'Chester'.

Instantly we have our sensory impressions: flashes from the ramparts as the sun catches the Roman's armour, eyes glinting through menacing metal hoods, the thump, thump, thump of marching feet.

All we need is a paragraph. We can grab a few children's books about the Romans from our local library and one, at least, will provide some evocative images we can work with (adult books tend to be too factual). The resulting paragraph might even replace the beginning paragraph of our family history, shunting that dry sentence further down the page, or even off it altogether.

But, you might argue, Chester's history has nothing to do with the family we are researching. True, the fort was founded a millennium before the surname period, but as the place-name evolved from its role as a Roman fort and as the surname developed from its connection with the place-name, ignoring the history of Chester would be to ignore the history of the surname. Moreover, we would miss out on the powerful sensory images that grip our readers' interest, the words that bring history to life.

Add a bit of information about the Anglo-Saxons (via the same sort of children's history books) and the Normans – a paragraph or two in total – and we have covered 1000 years to the surname period.

At this point we need to explore the history of Chester itself and try to find out what it was like in the Middle Ages, at the time when our Chester ancestor left there. We don't require a lot of information; again, a couple of paragraphs is probably enough.

Find some facts but again concentrate on the type of details that will evoke an image in our readers' minds. If a window in time opened and we could spy on Chester in the 1300s or 1400s, what would we see, what would we hear, what would we smell (it wouldn't be pleasant). Children's books talking about life in the Middle Ages can be helpful as well as some specific works relating to Chester itself.

Having completed these scene-setting paragraphs, we need to get our ancestors from Chester to wherever the first known member of our family lived.

> We pick up the Chester family in the year 1730 in Ullingswick parish, Herefordshire, some 75 miles south of Chester. When they left Chester and where they lived in the intervening centuries has not yet been established and will probably never be known.

Or, hopefully, something more exciting.

Thus, simply by examining our surname's origins, we have an interesting beginning to our family history. Moreover, this beginning places the family in its historical context – indeed it briefly covers nearly two millennia of British history – rather than having the Chester family appear from thin air as if a magician flicked his wand and, suddenly, they existed.

Locational names like Chester tell a story. We all love stories. If we seek the stories in all of our research, we cannot help but produce an interesting narrative.

Other surname-based beginnings

Personal names, occupational names: there are so many different ways we can introduce a family. Let me swing the pendulum to its extreme, using a nickname mentioned above.

In the same way that words communicate a perspective, they communicate a tone. Family histories don't need to be pompous and serious. If our surname of interest is a nickname, it could set the scene for a light-hearted jocular tone:

> Great-grandfather shouldn't have bothered trying to accrue wealth. With a surname like *Scattergood*, it wouldn't remain in the family's hands for long. Indeed, his son John 'scattered it good'. Evidently John had inherited the spendthrift ways of our long dead forebear, who was so renowned for his improvidence that our family has borne his unfortunate nickname for nearly a millennium.

With such a beginning, who wouldn't be keen to read on?

Commencing a family history with the surname's origin is merely one way to begin: logical but not essential. If this doesn't appeal, at least try to include information about the surname's origin somewhere in the early pages of the family history. The family has carried the surname for hundreds of years. Indeed, the surname has outlived every previous person who bore it. Don't ignore it as if it doesn't matter.

Pivotal events

What other ways can we begin our family histories? Perhaps there is a pivotal event in our ancestor's life, or in the backdrop history, that provides the perfect hook to dangle them from. When I wrote my Watson family history some decades ago, I started as follows:

> On 19 April 1775 at Lexington, Massachusetts, a band of American farmers faced a detachment of British soldiers. 'Disperse, ye rebels,' ordered the British commanding officer, but the farmers held their ground. They were angry, armed and determined. A shot was fired and a skirmish broke out. The American Revolution had begun.
>
> The first shot in the American Revolution, or War of Independence, has been immortalised as 'the shot heard round the world' as it marked the beginning of a war that changed

history. The war changed the lives of many individuals as well
... a young British soldier by the name of John Watson and his
descendants among them ...

Erik Larson began his bestselling *The Devil in the White City*
with the following paragraph:

> In Chicago at the end of the nineteenth century amid the smoke
> of industry and the clatter of trains there lived two men, both
> handsome, both blue-eyed and both unusually adept at their
> chosen skills. Each embodied an element of the great dynamic
> that characterised the rush of America towards the twentieth
> century. One was an architect, the builder of many of America's
> most important structures, among them the Flatiron Building in
> New York ...; the other was a murderer, one of the most prolific
> in history and harbinger of the American archetype, the urban
> serial killer. Although the two never met, their fate was linked
> by a single, magical event ...

Each of these introductions is like the top of an hour-glass. We
begin with the broad context then narrow to the family or person
of interest. The conclusion should be like the bottom of an hour-
glass, expanding out to cover the broad context again.

Hook their interest

The first sentence or paragraph in any work is nicknamed 'the
hook'. We can hook our readers' interest with that commencing
sentence or we can bore them so they chuck our book away.
Publishers and literary agents don't judge a book by its cover.
They judge it by that first sentence. If it's decent and they are in
a good mood, they'll read the first paragraph or the first page or
maybe the first chapter, but that's all. If it's poorly written, the
manuscript is tossed into the reject bin.

Some hooks are so potent they become part of our vernacular.
Think about one of the most famous hooks in history. Martin
Luther King Jr said:

> I have a dream ...

And that dream was so powerful that four decades later America had a black president.

A woman once sent me a link to a self-published ebook. She had stumbled across an intriguing story while researching her family history and it involved a famous poet – a name we all know – and a murder. As it turned out, I didn't get past the first line. She failed to hook me. She had started the book 'John Smith (or whoever) was born on ... ' And it continued in the same vein thereafter. What a wasted opportunity.

The prologue of my first popular history began with three simple sentences that evidently hooked the publisher:

> A menacing courtroom. A judge donning the dreaded black cap. A prisoner cowed.

This beginning seems dramatic and evocative yet essentially it is just a generic description of a criminal facing a death sentence. Anyone writing about a criminal ancestor has drama begging to be evoked. Give it a voice. Short sharp sentences like these are a powerful vehicle for doing so.

The other important place to hook our readers' interest is at the end of a chapter. Most readers read for a short period at night until they finish a chapter then put the book down. The books that are never finished are those that are not picked up again. But if we hook our reader at the end of a chapter, they will either keep reading or will be keen to get back to the book as soon as they can.

The prologue to *Breaking the Bank* ended with a question:

> Who had the effrontery to commit such a crime in a penal settlement, of all places?

The prologue to *Chubbie Miller* ended with something curious:

> Yet Lindbergh's flight didn't directly trigger the transformation in her life that began a few weeks later. Instead, it was something so small, so mundane, so ridiculously prosaic as a pat of butter.

To answer the question raised in readers' minds (how could a pat of butter change someone's life?), they have to keep reading.

The body of the introduction

Treat this introductory section as an overview of the family history, covering any important 'big picture' issues. For example, we could mention that the first three generations of the Chester family resided in Ullingswick, then the family gradually headed east towards London before splitting up and emigrating to Australia and America. We could conclude by saying that our last family member to carry the Chester surname was a woman named Mary Ann Chester who was our great-great-great-grandmother, or whatever.

Again, try to make it interesting rather than just dry and factual.

Summary

In my family history writing seminars, I often ask students to identify the most important sentence in a book. Almost everyone gets it right. The first sentence.

Then I ask what the second most important sentence is. Almost everyone gets it wrong. They say, 'The last sentence.' In fact, it's the second sentence.

Then I ask what the third most important sentence is. By this time, they are getting the message.

A reader starts at the start and keeps going (I won't mention those literary defilers who read the last page first). So if we cannot keep them interested enough to read past the first page, they will not reach the last page.

Unfortunately, it is rare for family members to read an entire family history. They will do so, though, if we bring their ancestors to life and write such an engaging narrative that they are eager to keep reading.

10

Words on the page

The easiest way to eat an elephant – or to deal with any other overwhelming task – is one bite at a time. It's helpful advice for writing a family history and for life in general.

Getting started

To begin crafting each biography, we can start the easy way with a chronological approach. We open a Word file (or whichever word-processing package we use) and type in the simple chapter headings mentioned in chapter seven; that is, Introduction, Researching the Family, Family 1: John Chester and Mary Ann Lang, and so on.

We place our files of Chester family information on the desk next to us, open the first file, pick up the first certificate or page of research notes, and read whatever is written. Then we turn the details into a simple sentence or paragraph that we type into the relevant chapter. Getting started is as simple as that.

It is essential that we don't attempt to craft beautiful prose at this time. In fact, one of the worst things we can do is polish our prose too early. Inevitably we will find information that requires us to completely rewrite the sentence or paragraph or even chapter. It is agony dumping a great sentence, even when it's no longer correct. The urge not to do so is very strong – as I can tell you from bitter personal experience.

While undertaking this process, commence a task list. Open a new computer file or go to a fresh page in a notebook and name it 'Task List'. It is helpful to jot down any thoughts or questions triggered by the information we have just written about – perhaps research that needs to be done or background reading that might prove useful. Note every idea. These are the leads we will follow to help make our family history more interesting.

The Chester family moved east from Ullingswick to London, with some stops along the way. How did they travel? If their journey was in the 1840s, for example, they possibly travelled by train. Examine maps. Make a task-list reminder to read railway history books to determine where train tracks had been laid, and whether train travel was likely and, if so, what these early train trips were like. Charles Dickens hated train travel: dirty, noisy and much too fast.

Just as an aside, it is worth remembering that contemporary fiction is often a better source of evocative information than general history books. The complete works of many of the masters are online and are searchable by words or phrases of interest. I stumbled across an intriguing piece of information while researching one of my books. In *Great Expectations*, Dickens' protagonist Pip lived with his uncle at the village smithy in Chalk, Kent, during the 1810s. This was the same timeframe in which the step-father of one of my protagonists was the village blacksmith at Chalk. We never know what we will find.

Having extracted our first sentence or paragraph from our research notes and typed it into the appropriate chapter, we need to source-reference the information.

Source referencing

UNSUBSTANTIATED HISTORY IS MYTHOLOGY!

I don't know who first wrote this, but thank-you. It should be the mantra of every genealogist and historian.

Documenting source references is boring at best and frustrating for those who don't know how. But unless we source-reference our material, we might as well be writing fiction. The easiest way to approach this task is to do it as we go along. If we note our source references from the start, we will always know where our information came from, even if it takes ten years to finish our family history.

Footnotes and Endnotes

A footnote allows us to add notes at the foot of a page, whereas an endnote adds notes in a special section at the end of a publication. Use footnotes or endnotes to source-reference the information found in original records; that is, information extracted from a baptism entry, census return, obituary, will, and so on.

Which should we use for source-referencing: a footnote or an endnote? Many academics use footnotes so their readers can instantly see the source references. In family histories, I prefer to use endnotes for source-referencing and footnotes for explanatory notes – for example, to explain the meaning of a word that is no longer in use. Including such information as a footnote saves the reader from having to constantly flip to the back of the book to find explanatory details.

Some authors use endnotes for both explanatory information and source-referencing details. The drawback is that readers cannot tell which is which so they are forced to check every annotation just in case it contains elaborations. If we annotate every piece of research, as we should, our readers will soon give up checking.

One way we can reduce the total number of endnotes is to include a single endnote number at the end of each paragraph. This links to an endnote that contains all the sources used to generate that paragraph.

If we are using footnotes as well as endnotes, we will need to distinguish between them. For example, we might use letters for footnotes (a, b, c) which begin again on each page. We might use numbers for endnotes (1, 2, 3) which begin again each chapter. While a single consecutive string of endnote references is easier for the reader, a large annotated family history can have thousands of endnote source-references. The resulting long numbers[1345] against each source-reference[1346] are extremely distracting[1347] and soon tire even the most committed reader.

Inserting footnotes or endnotes by computer is easy and can usually be done via the top-bar menu. There is no excuse for leaving out source references. And why would we want to, anyway, when we have made such an effort to find the information in the first place, which our source references prove. Unsource-referenced family histories are not only unprofessional, they are extremely frustrating for those who want to know where the information came from and how reliable it is.

Source-referencing guidelines

Many family historians don't know how to properly source-reference books or journals or original records. The book by Elizabeth Shown Mills listed in the 'book' source reference below is the source-referencing bible for genealogists and historians. Otherwise, some simple source-referencing tips are shown below.

For a book:

Mills, Elizabeth Shown *Evidence Explained: Citing History Sources from Artifacts to Cyberspace*, Genealogical Publishing Co., Baltimore, 2012

For an edited book:

Baxter, Carol J. (ed.) *General Musters of New South Wales, Norfolk Island and Van Diemen's Land 1811*, Australian Biographical and Genealogical Record, Sydney, 1987

For a journal article:

Baxter, Carol 'Musters of NSW from 1800 – Part 2' in *Descent* Vol. 29 Part 4 (December 1999), pp.194-200

Original records

Original records vary in nature. Pick a referencing style and stick to it. For example, the first, third and fifth examples below go from broad to narrow, documenting the record type first and the individual last. It is best to abbreviate the record repository references to reduce page length and therefore money. A repository key is listed below.

For an original record:

Convict Indent – *Earl Cornwallis* 1801: Sarah Pearce [SRNSW ref: 4/4004 p.296; Fiche 630]; or

Earl Cornwallis 1801 – Convict Indent: Sarah Pearce [SRNSW ref: 4/4004 p.296; Fiche 630]

Birth Certificate: John Pearce, 1860 [RBDM-NSW ref: 1860/2534]; or

John Pearce: Birth Certificate 1860 [RBDM-NSW ref: 1860/2534]

Letter: John Stephen Jnr to Governor Darling, 29 Apr 1829 [ML ref: MSS 836 p.36; Reel CY 905]

Repository key:

ML	Mitchell Library, Sydney, NSW
RBDM-NSW	Registry of Births, Deaths & Marriages, NSW
SRNSW	State Records of New South Wales, NSW.

Bibliography versus Endnotes

When we exhaustively research our biographical subject, most of our endnote references come from original records. Occasionally we will extract information about our biographical subject from a history book or family history. The publication's full source reference is included in the bibliography. That being the case, we don't need to provide the publication's full source reference in our endnote reference. 'Baxter, *Black Widow*, p.91' will suffice.

However, it is essential that we attempt to locate the original source for any information found in an authored work. If we rely on another's research, we are implicitly assuming that they are skilled and honest researchers. Be warned. Not only are there poorly skilled genealogists and historians, there are also rogue family historians, those who have little concern with the truth but are more interested in pandering to their own egos.

Do not provide endnote source-references for general background information. For example, regarding the background information about the Romans who established the fort at Chester, simply list in the bibliography the publications that were used.

Getting started (continued)

Having typed the information from our first page of research notes into our Word file, added any thoughts into our task list, and added a source reference via an endnote and/or a bibliographic reference, it is time to mark off the document as having been processed. I put a red tick in the top right-hand corner and file it appropriately. Of course, be careful about marking original records.

Thus, not only have we begun to write our family history, we are efficiently processing and filing our research – a double benefit.

One of the best pieces of advice I received as a beginner genealogist was to write research results on loose-leaf notepads, one person or one surname to a single-sided page. The individual pages can be slipped into manila folders, each storing information that relates to one surname or one person only. When it is time to write up these research results or to re-assess them, it is easy to find every piece of information for our person of interest because it is all in the one place.

Having fully processed the first document, we pick up the next document and add the details to our biography. We position the information before or after the previous information as is chronologically appropriate.

Then we keep going, one document at a time, patiently, meticulously typing all of our research results into the relevant 'chapter' on our computer, adding source references, and filing the original material. We don't need to group our research results into sections before we start typing because we do so as we go along. For now, the most important exercise is to get the words onto the page.

Planner or pantser

Psychologically, this strategy for writing up research may not work for you. Under Ann Curthoys and Ann McGrath's guidelines in *How to write history that people want to read*, I am classified as a *data dumper*. And also a *write-early historian*. Books on writing refer to me as a 'seat-of-the-pants' writer or a *pantser*.

You, however, might be a *staged writer*, one who does all the research then writes each section methodically. Or you might be a *padding historian*, one who structures a loose biographical framework then starts to fill in the details. Or you might be an *over-diligent researcher* who is likely to keep researching forever because you can't bear to start writing until you've gathered EVERY piece of information. I suspect there are many over-diligent family historians around, not so much because they are obsessively diligent but because it is the perfect strategy to put off the seemingly overwhelming task of starting to write.

Whatever you are, just do something. Take the first bite of that elephant. It really isn't the size of the universe, although it might seem so at this moment.

Annotated timeline

If you are planning to write a family history that is strongly narrative rather than detail-heavy, yet you wish to include the detail somewhere, I strongly suggest including an annotated timeline in the publication for each biographical subject.

While it is desirable to source-reference every piece of primary-source information so that others can find it again, it is sometimes unwise to do so because endnote annotations can be jarring. This is the case in publications aimed at the broader market like my own popular histories.

In my first popular history, I included *blind endnotes* at the end of the publication; that is, I listed the chapter number then the sources in usage order.

In the second, *Breaking the Bank*, I included annotated timelines for each important character, sixteen in all. These enabled me to include every fact I had found for the relevant individuals along with the associated source references and to include analytical or explanatory information where necessary. I was then able to omit the excessive detail from the narrative, the detail that bogs down the narrative and bores the reader.

I prepared annotated timelines for the third, *Captain Thunderbolt and his Lady*, but found that they were too large for the book. There is so much controversy associated with the Thunderbolt legend that I built a website (www.thunderboltbushranger.com. au) and included the timelines and analyses of the evidence on the website. As it costs a few hundred dollars annually to run the Thunderbolt website, I have not done the same for my later works. For these, I have included bibliographies in the publication containing original records and authored works.

In our annotated timelines, we can include a single line for every fact, or we can group information as otherwise seems relevant, as shown in the example on the next page.

An annotated timeline is also useful as a research-processing tool if we have a vast amount of material. In fact, it is not only useful, it is well-nigh essential. Documenting our research in this way helps us make sense of our ancestor's activities and movements, and reduce our chances of making a major blunder – as many a biographer has learnt to their cost.

Where should we position annotated timelines in a family history publication? They can either be added at the end of the chapter relating to our biographical subject, or as a group at the end of the publication.

Timeline for William Blackstone

1796 circa	Born London[1]
1815 pre	Whitesmith and founder residing London[2]
1815-16	13/14 Sep 1815: tried at Old Bailey Criminal Sessions for forging and coining and sentenced to 14 years' transportation; 11 Jan 1816: Transferred to *Justitia* hulk; 6 May: Transferred to *Mariner* transport; 11 Oct: Arrived Sydney per transport *Mariner*; 16 Oct: Disembarked from the *Mariner*[3]
...	
1828 Oct	7 Oct: Implicated in robbery; 22 Oct: Ordered to the *Phoenix* hulk; 23 Oct: Admitted to the hulk[4]

Endnotes

1. Convict Indents – *Mariner* 1816: William Blackstone [SRNSW ref: 4/4005 p.207; Fiche 636]; Certificate of Freedom: William Blackstone 1829 [SRNSW ref: 4/4299 No.29/0904; Reel 985]
2. Convict Indents – ibid
3. Convict Indents – ibid; The Proceedings of the Old Bailey: William Blackstone 13 Sep 1815 [http://www.oldbailyonline. org/html_units/1810s/t18150913-13.html]; Newgate Calendar – Middlesex Session commencing 13 Sep 1815 No.139: Arraignments, Verdicts and Judgements [TNA ref: HO 77/22]; Index to *Justitia* hulk [TNA ref: HO 9/5 No.1209; ML PRO Reel 4880]; *Justitia* Hulk Register [TNA ref: HO 9/4 p.13 No.1209; ML PRO Reel 4880]; Haslam *Narrative*
4. Bunn to Colonial Secretary's Office, 7 Oct 1828 [SRNSW ref: 4/1994 No.28/7959] & also Memorandum to Principal Supt of Police & Sheriff attached to previous letter; Colonial Secretary to Sheriff, 22 Oct 1828 [SRNSW ref: 4/3896 p.31 No.28/64; Reel 1062]

11

Words of wisdom

A book should have a beginning, middle and end, and so should a biography. Many family histories start a new biography for a person whose basic details were provided in a previous chapter yet don't repeat the details. Readers are forced to back-track to find relevant information: like when the person was born.

Family history readers
Here are some important points to remember when crafting our family histories:
1. Family members rarely read an entire family history in a single sitting – unless it's very short. It doesn't matter how interesting we make it, it is not a light novel.
2. There is a limit to how much any reader can absorb in one reading session, or remember if days or weeks pass before they return to reading the book.
3. Most family members will read the family history from cover to cover on only one or two occasions (if at all) and thereafter only read the chapters relating to their own ancestors.
4. Those interested in our family history because their ancestor's sibling or cousin married into the family will use our family history as a research tool. They will want to photocopy a specific chapter or chapters relating to their person of interest and would prefer that the relevant information is not scattered throughout the book forcing them to skim the whole book trying to find it (can you hear the tones of frustrated personal experience).

For all of these reasons, it is advisable to have each biography complete within itself. Naturally this will result in some repetition. If we explain our reasoning in the Introduction or in an Author's Note, we are covered.

Crafting biographies

Having documented all of our research in our Word file, we might decide to stick with a family history that is a series of consecutive biographies, as outlined in chapter seven. These biographies commence when the relevant person is born and finish when that person dies. This structure is the easiest to follow when writing self-published multi-generational family histories.

Alternatively, having documented all of our research and explored the background history, we might decide to be more creative. However, first we need to craft the biographies.

While our initial biographies – little more than information dumps at this stage – will have a chronological structure, we need to group information, to some extent at least. Otherwise the biographies will jump around too much. This is where computers make it so easy, allowing us to lift sections and move them to different places. For example, we could group information so that the biography discusses the couple's marriage and children's births in one section, business dealings in another, land purchases somewhere else, and so on, working within and around the simple chronology as we go.

Each paragraph needs to flow into the next so keep moving the paragraphs of information around until the structure hangs together neatly.

Thematic family histories

At this point we might notice that a strong theme runs through all the biographies – perhaps that of an enterprising spirit which reflected the developments of the Industrial Revolution. Instead of a simple complete-within-itself biographical structure, we might decide to loosen the structure and allow this theme to predominate. A thematically-based family history is more difficult to write but, if well done, is more interesting to read.

That being the case, we would need a link between chapters that maintains the theme – the through-line, in writing-speak – so that one person's life story flows into the next. A disjointed structure is truly painful for readers.

It is best if inexperienced writers do not attempt a thematically-based family history in their first attempt at writing history. I discuss this style further in *Writing and Publishing Gripping Family Histories*.

Don't delay

We will never find every surviving reference to our ancestors. Some researchers try to use the excuse that they haven't finished researching the family to justify not beginning to write their family history. We can start at any time and now is better than later.

And just think. If we are knocked over by a bus tomorrow, who would make head or tail of our notes? Most genealogists these days use genealogical programs but how many non-genealogists would have the patience to try and learn how they work. By the time another family member became interested in our research, the odds are that our computer would be long gone.

Which raises another point. It is important that we keep a print-out of everything we have written about our ancestors, just in case.

12

From dry to interesting

I used to joke that while most people managed to extract a paragraph of writing from the information in an original record like a birth certificate, I could write a page. I joke no longer. That skill helped launch my writing career.

Weave in the historical backdrop

It is surprisingly easy to write an entire page once we start thinking more broadly. Take the first piece of information on a birth certificate: the date. It is helpful to google the date and see if anything interesting happened that day in history. Examine history books. Try to discover what was happening around that time: in the world, in the country, in the town. Something might jump out.

For Sarah Adams, for example, with a date and a place, we could start as follows:

> As England rallied its troops to face the threat of a French invasion, Sarah Adams was born in Deal on the Strait of Dover, only 25 miles from the French seaport of Calais.

Drama; tension. Nothing is made up yet the reader wants to know more. Did the French invade? Did the English fight them off? What happened?

We slip in the details about Sarah's birth-date and baptism then turn our narrator eyeglass onto the town itself. We describe what the residents were doing to protect themselves: carting wood to the tops of hills to build beacons and construct barriers. We describe the red-coated soldiers marching through town, the sailor-packed warships tossing anchors overboard. We communicate the sense of fear that permeated these English coastal towns when the seemingly invincible Napoleon made camp at Boulogne with his cockily named Army of England and roared, 'Let us be masters of the Channel for six hours and we are masters of the world.' We let the reader see Sarah's world through our eyes, that is, the narrator's eyes. While these might not be Sarah's eyes, the effect is almost the same.

Weave in the locational backdrop

Perhaps nothing was happening at the relevant time, nothing that adds life to our family history anyway. Instead, we might focus our narrator eyeglass on what we do know: that our ancestor was baptised at a specific church, for example. It is not hard to find descriptive information about pre-twentieth century churches. Use these details to communicate the facts in a way that the reader can visualise and experience:

> On 24 March 1799 Sarah's parents carried her up to the little stone church perched on top of the hill ...

Write active rather than passive history

By describing Sarah's baptism in this way, we are making our ancestors active participants in their own story, in our narrative. We are, in fact, writing history in the *active voice narrative* rather than the usual *passive voice narrative*. This is similar, in the big picture, to writing active sentences rather than passive sentences, which is discussed further in chapter sixteen.

The passive version would be: 'On 24 March 1799 Sarah was baptised ...'. But this intimates that she miraculously appeared in the church and was baptised without anyone doing anything. Is that the truth? Of course not. The reality is that her parents – or someone else – had to get her to the church and a cleric had to perform the baptismal ceremony. So why can't we say the following:

The clergyman dipped his hand into the centuries-old engraved font then splashed holy water across her brow, intoning the words that would usher her into God's grace.

Background information as well as logic and imagination are essential in writing active history. In this instance, we are using information about the church and the traditional baptismal ceremony to turn the simple facts written in the church register – the words that document an actual event – into the event itself. Why shouldn't we give ourselves permission to communicate the reality of the baptism experience rather than hiding behind a bland recitation of the supposed facts?

Is this fictionalising history. No, it is not. We haven't put words in their mouths or thoughts in their heads. We haven't described the husband looking out the window or the wife smoothing back her hair or the cleric tripping over the altar. That would indeed be fictionalising our family histories.

But, you might say, how can we know that her parents carried her to the church? Someone else might have done so. Well, logic and probability suggest that her parents took her to the church (how often does someone else take an infant to be baptised). Moreover, we can never know otherwise because the information isn't documented. Thus, in the same way that we have to assume that the 'facts' in the church register are correct, we can allow our ancestors to live these facts.

Instead of the date of birth and date of baptism being the dominant information in this section of Sarah's biography, they are merely the foundation stones. Or perhaps 'stepping stones' is a better description as we use them to step onto a path, perhaps well-trodden, perhaps not. Wherever the path leads, we can be certain that the destination will be much more interesting than the bald listing of the date or the place that we began with.

Think about the child

The child's given name comes next on the birth certificate. *Sarah*, for example, is a biblical name, Hebrew for 'princess', the wife of *Abraham*, 'the patriarch'. One of the most common female names in Sarah Adams' time, it has a timeless elegance and has retained its popularity. Was it a family name bestowed upon her in honour of her mother or grandmother?

What about the child's place in the family? Where did Sarah Adams herself fit in? Was she the bossy eldest child who took responsibility for her family in times of trouble, or perhaps the spoilt baby of the family who felt the world owed her? Sometimes we can glimpse character in surviving records, although character is usually communicated through letters and pictures rather than sources that merely provide names and dates. Whatever the source, the word *perhaps* is useful – sometimes essential – when making such speculations.

Think about the parents

What about the child's parents? The details in a baptism entry or birth certificate can also serve as stepping stones to more interesting information. For example, to simply write 'Sarah Adams' father was a blacksmith' and then move on to the next fact is to waste an ideal opportunity.

'Under a spreading chestnut tree,' wrote Longfellow in *A Village Blacksmith*:

> The village smithy stands;
> The smith, a mighty man is he,
> With large and sinewy hands.
> And the muscles of his brawny arm
> Are strong as irons bands ...

With these lines we instantly evoke an image of a blacksmith in our readers' minds. It doesn't matter that it isn't Sarah Adams' father. All blacksmiths had sinewy hands and muscles of iron.

Instead of quoting the poem (duly acknowledged if we do so), we could paraphrase the sensory images: the roar of the bellows, the beat of the heavy sledge, the flaming forge, the flying sparks. This was the world of Sarah's youth and Longfellow helps bring it to life for our readers.

If we can't evoke powerful images with our own words, we can use the classics to help us. The masters' voices can echo through our family history, bringing vividness and beauty without breaching copyright laws or plagiarism norms.

Weave in more history

Sarah Adams' biography mentioned her marriage in July 1815. Here's more fodder for our historical searches. We learn that Sarah was married just a few weeks after Britain won the Battle of Waterloo, ending two decades of hostilities with the French.

For the whole of Sarah's life, England had been at war. Imagine what it must have been like when the news reached the nation, when its people realised the implications of this momentous victory.

But we don't need to use our imagination. We can easily discover Britain's reaction by reading general history books and online newspapers. These sources communicate the excitement that flooded the nation.

Our ancestors were not insulated from their times. They were participants. History doesn't happen on its own. People make history. So we must not ignore the times simply because we don't know for certain about our ancestors' involvement, about what they thought or said or did. We just need to communicate the mood of the nation:

> The country rejoiced. Triangular wooden-frames set with candles appeared in England's windows, crowds danced in the streets, gunshots rang out, rockets soared, and its citizens flocked to churches of every denomination offering prayers of thanksgiving.

Explore the social context

English marriage registers from 1754 onwards along with Scottish and Catholic baptism registers and most birth, marriage and death certificates include the names of witnesses or godparents. Unless these people were family members, most genealogists merely list the names in their family histories or ignore them altogether. Yet these witnesses can provide fascinating insights into our ancestor's social community.

The female protagonist for my third book was the child of an English-born convict father and an Aboriginal mother. That simple piece of information listed on her baptism entry isn't just the source of a paragraph or page of information, but potentially multiple chapters reflecting Aboriginal history, British settlement, frontier conflict and so on.

Just to make an interesting story even more intriguing, the woman's sister married a 'Chinaman'. The witnesses were listed as: 'Signature in Chinese – English Ungpe' and 'Ellen Ungpe'. Instantly we can envisage a subset within the community: a group of Chinese men with 'white' or 'black' wives. Writing about attitudes to the Chinese and to the women who married Chinese men, and trying to determine the number of similar families in the area, will make a more interesting family history than just listing the names of the marriage witnesses.

Explore causes of death

The only thing we can be sure about when tracing our family history is that, at some point or another, everyone kicks the bucket. So rather than simply writing that so-and-so died on such-and-such a date and was buried two days later at such-and-such a cemetery, how can we make it interesting without being morbid or melodramatic or unctuously sentimental?

Death certificates and obituaries can provide useful insights into people's lives by recording their causes of death. Perhaps the person died from a disease that is no longer prevalent. If so, their cause of death provides an opportunity to explore the historical context. For example, puerperal fever – otherwise known as childbed fever – was a major cause of maternal deaths in past centuries whereas in western countries today it is uncommon and rarely deadly, thanks to antibiotics. Of course, there were no antibiotics in those days and few sources of pain-relief. In fact, the moment a woman realised she was pregnant, she lived with a pervading fear – would she survive childbirth?

Today we congratulate mothers-to-be, but in the past pregnancy was a source of mixed emotions. Joy for a first-time mother no doubt, mixed with a fear that increased as her baby's birth approached. Joy for a second-time mother, and maybe a third. But what about a poor woman pregnant for the fourth, fifth, sixth ... dozenth time? Think of the exhaustion of being constantly pregnant or night-feeding an infant; sleep-deprivation is a form of torture yet most women endured it for twenty or thirty years. Think of the demands of feeding another mouth. Just feeding one mouth was, in relative terms, more expensive than today. Feeding a dozen? Obesity was only a problem for the well-to-do, rickets a prevailing problem for the poor.

So if we know nothing about a woman other than that she mothered a dozen children or died from a child-birth related disease, yet we want to provide some sense of her, we can think about these life – and death – experiences.

Sometimes multiple members of a family died from the same cause of death, providing a theme for the family history or at least a link between chapters.

When writing about the cause of death itself, let's not bore everyone with a clinical description: 'Bright's is a type of kidney disease ...' We are not writing encyclopaedia entries. I happened to read a fascinating book about one particular disease which led me to write the following:

> The White Plague of Europe was one of the malady's many nicknames. The disease would kill a billion humans worldwide in the nineteenth and twentieth centuries alone. Indeed, it was the biggest killer ever of humankind, perhaps first appearing with the origins of life itself, apparently reaching epidemic proportions in the ancient world's majestic cities, bequeathed, along with civilisation itself, to the rest of humanity yet not restricted to humans alone, eating away at bones and lungs, swelling neck glands into pus-filled protrusions, thickening and

reddening facial skin until it developed a wolf-like appearance, killing more than half its victims within five years and one in seven of the world's total population, a never-ending epidemic that having arrived uninvited on a nation's doorstep refused ever to leave.

In writing terms, this paragraph is called a 'cascade': one sentence that builds upon its theme, that unfolds in stages without being exhausting in the way that overly long sentences usually are. And because it doesn't say what the disease was, the reader is intrigued and keeps reading. So what is the disease?

Tuberculosis: the greatest story never told by Frank Ryan is not only a fascinating story; it is beautifully written. Considering that one-seventh of the world's population – including many of our ancestors – died from this dreadful disease, the book is worth reading.

Perhaps we might be able to find information about the likely course of our ancestor's disease so as to gain a sense of his suffering, of what led him to prepare a 'last will and testament' signed with a shaky signature three weeks before his death.

Summary

Each of these suggestions is merely a path we can follow if we choose to do so. We might already have copious information for a person who had a common occupation or died from a common complaint, in which case there is little need to explore these areas any further. Elaborating on the cause of death, for example, is particularly useful when it was a long-term complaint that would have impacted upon a person's life, or when we know very little else about them. It helps bring them to life – even in death.

13

The dramatic experience

It is a truth not universally acknowledged that, for a genealogist at least, a bad ancestor is more interesting than a good one. While we as a society aspire to goodness, the good souls slip through history largely unnoticed. But the baddies, duck and weave as they might, still manage to get caught in history's baleful glare.

In the previous chapter, we began with a couple of simple primary-source references – a baptism and marriage entry – and by finding general historical information we were able to flesh out the story. The truly dramatic material is found in the criminal records.

Writing drama

'Upon the 27th of October,' testified Richard Down Esq. at the Old Bailey trial of Charles Peat in 1781, 'the prisoner at the bar stopped my carriage upon Finchley common and demanded my money.'

'Was he on horseback?' asked the Court.

'Yes,' replied Down.

'Was he alone?'

'Yes,' Down said again. 'I gave him my purse. Says he, 'If you value your purse, you will please to take it back and give me the contents of it,' and he returned my purse. The prisoner refused my watch. He saw it. He said he was an unfortunate man and only wanted a little money and behaved throughout with remarkable civility. While I was taking the money out of my purse, my servant that was behind the carriage jumped on behind him on his horse. My servant clasped him round the body and brought him to the ground. I immediately got behind my servant to secure him and with some difficulty we did so. I put him in my carriage and drove him to Colney-hatch.'

Wonderful stuff.

The Old Bailey session papers are full of such accounts of London trials. While the transcripts of county trials have rarely survived, local newspapers often provide detailed descriptions of the original criminal activity and the resulting court case.

If the case was important, newspapers across the country sometimes provided almost verbatim transcripts of victim and witness testimonies, with each report varying slightly depending upon how fast the correspondent could take notes and how many column-inches the newspaper devoted to the case. When we sift through all the reports and extract any new pieces of information, we can end up with an astonishingly detailed account of a crime and its aftermath. In *Chubbie Miller*, I have eighteen chapters devoted to a death and a sensational Florida murder trial. All of the information came from contemporary newspaper reports because the trial transcripts have not survived.

There are three ways to write about criminal activity or any other physical activity we come across in our research:

1. We can briefly paraphrase the account:

    > On 27 October 1781, highwayman Charles Peat stopped a carriage on Finchley common and demanded money from the owner Richard Down Esq. ...

    Boring!

2. We can tell the story of the crime through the victim and witness testimonies at the resulting court-case, as shown at the start of this chapter. The account reads almost like fiction yet it is simply extracted from the trial transcript with some judicious editing and the addition of dialogue tags like *asked* and *replied*.

    We can craft an even better description if we set the scene,

as any good fiction writer must do, without making it up.
In this situation, we could bring the reader with us into the
courtroom:

> Inside the Old Bailey gallery, spectators jockeyed for
> position, trying to get to the front so they could gaze down at
> the prisoner-lined dock and at the bench where a wigged and
> robed judge presided. Strategically positioned on the wall
> behind the judge was a huge sword capped with a crown,
> symbolic of the state's supreme power over life and death
> – a mighty Sword of Damocles about to plunge through the
> unworthy, and a timely reminder that this wasn't merely
> a form of theatrical entertainment. Festive flowers lay on
> one side of the judge: an air freshener to camouflage the
> prisoners' stench. A pile of herbs sat on the other: a quaint
> fumigant intended to dispel the deadly prisoner fever,
> typhus. It was another timely reminder: that death stalked
> all of those who entered the courthouse.

Books about the Old Bailey and pictures of the court-room
itself provided the sources for the above information.

3. We can tell the story of the crime as if it is happening at
this moment or has just happened. Trial transcripts provide
action, description and dialogue yet these are rarely used to
their greatest advantage by family historians. Considerably
more information was included in Richard Down's testimony
and those of his two servants and we can use all of these
details, with the addition of logic and imagination, to make
an exciting story:

> It was nearing 5 pm when Richard Down Esq. steered his
> carriage off the main road and onto Finchley Common. He
> was travelling from London to his country house and was
> almost at the seven-mile stone when a horse loomed out of
> the gathering darkness ...

As often as possible, we should let the victims and witnesses live their own stories while we paint a vivid word picture of the backdrop. Writing history or family history in this way might seem an unusual approach yet in many ways it brings us closer to the true historical experience.

The true historical experience

Historians do not have time-warp binoculars that allow them to view the past as if watching a movie. A simple historical account draws upon numerous individual experiences. The historian extracts the necessary details and sifts out biases (where recognised) to produce a running account.

In doing so, however, the resulting account can lose the immediacy of the personal accounts it was drawn from. Getting back to the roots of history, that is, letting the participants tell their own stories, will make our family histories more vivid and alive and genuinely interesting.

Writing dialogue

If we think about the 'normal' approach to writing history, we realise that most historians ignore much of the material that brings life to a narrative – such as dialogue. We generally think of dialogue as a tool of fiction however dialogue abounds in historical records. For example, when victims or witnesses testify in a criminal trial, they frequently recount conversations they had with the perpetrator or others: 'I said ... then he said ...'. This is our dialogue.

If we put the words in the mouths of the participants at the time of the event in question and weave a picture of the setting, we have a scene that reads like fiction. It is not fiction yet our readers will be as gripped as if it were.

> 'How are you getting on?' Dingle asked, and some idle conversation followed as the men carefully scanned their surroundings. Dingle then whispered to Blackstone, 'Will you be one of a party to rob the Bank of Australia?'
> Astonished, Blackstone scoffed, 'It is impossible to be

done! It is a foolish idea!'

'When you hear my plan you will think otherwise,' Dingle assured him. 'It is easily to be done.'

We can tell that the dialogue isn't made up because the phraseology is different to that of today – and to how fiction writers imagine people spoke in the past. I extracted this dialogue from depositions and testimonies. Then I thought about the words used and the likely tone of voice and added appropriate dialogue tags. They weren't hard to choose. Think about it. If someone suggested we rob a bank and we responded with Blackstone's words (as recounted by Blackstone himself), aren't we revealing astonishment in a scathingly dismissive tone? Isn't Dingle's response one of assurance or re-assurance?

Just as an aside, it is best not to quote huge slabs of dialogue from court records or letters, or even huge slabs in general, because readers will usually skip them. Judicious editing is always advisable. If required, the full text can be included in an appendix.

Even if we don't have court-room testimonies to draw upon, we can pull dialogue of one form or another from many different types of original records.

'We have sold everything we possessed and at this period I am overwhelmed with the most distressing calamity for I have no other means of supporting my family,' Thomas Turner wrote to the governor, begging to be allowed the freedom to work for himself.

Dialogue can communicate drama and tension, humour and pathos, and most significantly character:

'Can I have a plate of bread and cheese and a glass of brandy and water?' asked the rabid teetotaller.

That simple line of dialogue combined with the dialogue tag 'asked the rabid teetotaller' communicates the hypocrisy of the protagonist. Think of the difference if the dialogue tag had simply said 'asked John'.

And what about the next example? The 'dialogue' here is taken from a woman's letter to her husband, the above-mentioned rabid teetotaller. The 'dialogue tag' begins the paragraph:

> There was a poignancy in her final words: 'The year has opened with a lovely day. I hope it is an omen of the future which awaits us.'

On the very day she wrote that letter, her husband killed his mistress. It is important to think carefully about the words we use as our dialogue tags. These words must link our quote with the preceding and following information so the narrative flows seamlessly. Ideally, they should also add depth to the material being quoted. They are most likely to do so when the author makes an authorial judgement.

Authorial judgements

Most family historians simply provide the facts and some additional description and rarely examine character. Even though we have all heard the truisms that we shouldn't judge books by their covers and that beauty is only skin deep, family historians rarely look beyond the surface.

It is critical that family historians realise that their role is to do more than simply present the facts. As historian Hannah Farnham Lee wrote:

> A mere compilation of facts presents only the skeleton of History; we do but little for her if we cannot invest her with life, clothe her in the habiliments of her day, and enable her to call forth the sympathies of succeeding generations.

It is so apt and so beautifully written, we should perhaps print it out and affix it to the wall near our computer to remind us when we start writing.

Imagine reading a novel that only included facts and description. We'd get bored very quickly. What about celebrity biographies? Our interest is pricked when authors communicate their sense of their subject, their judgment about the person's actions. Unauthorised celebrity biographies generally sell better than authorised biographies because the reader gets to hear what the author truly thinks.

Characterisation is critical to our appreciation of both fiction and professionally-written biographies. This is because our characters are the engines that drive us as human beings. Thus it is essential that we try to examine character when writing our family histories. We need to communicate a sense of our ancestors as human beings with real emotions and real character flaws.

To invest history with life, we must therefore – to some extent at least – make judgements about the people we are writing about. We are the ones researching and writing our family histories. We are the experts. We have the knowledge that allows us to form opinions about our family's actions and activities. True, in many cases we will lack enough information to do so. However, it is amazing what judgments we can make and what conclusions we can draw from even the simplest information.

Look at the last two examples in the 'writing dialogue' section above. The reference to John Tawell as a 'rabid teetotaller' reveals my authorial judgement that he was being a hypocrite. The suggestion that his wife's letter communicated poignancy reflects another authorial judgement.

Most genealogists seem to be too afraid to make these sorts of judgements in case they get them wrong. The important point to remember is that there is no 'right' or 'wrong'. Authorial judgements are opinions. And the communication of that opinion makes the prose much more interesting to read.

What judgements can we make about our ancestors? It takes courage to decide to uproot one's family and travel across the world's oceans to settle in a new land. While it might also reflect desperation, think of all the desperate people who stayed at home.

And for those with criminal ancestors, it takes audacity to shoplift whereas embezzlement is a sly furtive crime. Murder usually reflects a brutality in the murderer's nature, a lack of empathy for those they have targeted.

Generating reader emotions

When we look beyond the surface to character, we are taking the first step along the path towards generating an emotional response in our readers. If we can elicit an emotional response, our readers will be keen to read on. If we can elicit anger or fear in particular, we have tapped into the reptilian part of their brains, the amygdala. It is a sign that our readers are completely immersed in our narrative. It is a sign that our readers are hooked.

One of the best ways to generate emotions in our readers is to *show* them rather than *tell* them what is happening.

Show don't tell

We don't need to force-feed our readers. We don't have to *tell* them everything. It is better if we let them use their own imaginations and intelligence to work it out. That's one of the thrills of reading crime novels – trying to work out what is going on before the author reveals all.

Remember when the rabid teetotaller asked for alcohol? I could have *told* readers that 'John Tawell was a hypocrite.' Instead I *showed* them using the sentence of dialogue taken from a newspaper report and the dialogue tag.

'Show don't tell' is an important mantra for all writers. We should repeat these words whenever we sit down to write. 'Show don't tell!'

This subject is discussed further in *Writing and Publishing Gripping Family Histories*.

Stream of consciousness writing

Most genealogists don't have the benefits of information from newspaper reports and personal correspondence. Indeed, we often have little more than dry facts. One of the ways we can make dry facts more interesting is to use a stream-of-consciousness style of writing. Here is an example.

When I researched *An Irresistible Temptation*, I discovered that Jane New was convicted of shoplifting. I had no newspaper reports or trial transcripts to tell me what she was doing or how she was caught, nothing except the brief court report of her conviction. However, I also discovered that she had continued to shoplift when she had no need for the money. This indicates that, for Jane, there was more to the shoplifting experience than necessity alone. Something else was driving her.

I wanted to write about what might have been motivating her yet I couldn't say what she did or thought or felt because that specific information hadn't survived. And I couldn't make it up because I wasn't writing fiction. However, I did have information about the general shoplifting experience. This included a report from a French female psychologist written in the 1890s which talked about a middle-class woman's urge to shoplift. My challenge was to use this information to communicate Jane's experience without fictionalising the account. This is the result:

> As later financial independence failed to curb her shoplifting pursuits, she must have become enthralled by the sense of exhilaration it gave her. The delicious feeling of anticipation upon venturing into a store, of crossing into 'their' world. The heightened sense of awareness, of watching out for an opportunity while concealing her intentions. The focusing of attention on a particular object which pulled her in, wanting to be possessed. The sleight of hand required to grasp and hide the object. The ruse allowing her to escape undetected. The satisfaction at having achieved a successful violation of the rules both moral and legal that shackled her to a tedious existence.

It comes across as if we are seeing her commit the crime even though this is not specifically stated.

How is this achieved? Note that all except the first sentence are incomplete. They lack a *subject* (from the subject-verb-object perspective). At no point does this paragraph actually say what

Jane was thinking or feeling or doing yet this type of stream-of-consciousness writing makes it appear that way.

This is another technique we can use to draw the reader into the world inhabited by our characters without resorting to fictionalising our family histories.

14

Scenic experiences

It is amazing how many family histories refer to a town or village without providing any information about it:

> Sarah Adams was born in Deal, Kent, on 1 February 1799 to John Adams, a blacksmith, and his wife Mary, nee Jones. She was baptised on 24 March 1799 at St Mary's Church of England, Deal. On 29 July 1815 she married ...

Like a good novelist, we must set the scene either before we introduce Sarah or soon afterwards.

It is easy to find information about towns. Most towns are the subject of at least one book. And information usually abounds on the internet, accessible either through a general search or a Google Books search.

Villages can prove harder to find information about. For those tracing a British family, Samuel Lewis' *Topographical Dictionaries* are helpful. They provide information about every parish, town and village in England, Scotland, Ireland and Wales in the 1830/40s. The population statistics he mentions are extracted from the contemporaneous British census returns. The census abstracts themselves record population statistics from 1801 onwards, a useful guide to the size of our ancestor's community. Many Australian state libraries provide access to these via the on-line Parliamentary Papers. Other countries might provide a similar access.

The *Statistical Accounts of Scotland* record a snapshot of each Scottish parish in the 1790s and again in the 1830/40s. Sometimes they include a dozen pages of information for just a tiny parish.

These publications can prove a goldmine for those researching a Scottish family.

Use these sources to find the facts as well as information that provides a visual description. Arthur Mee's *King's England* series, which described his journeys through England's counties in the first half of the twentieth century, can help us picture the environment. Similar publications can be found from the 1600s onwards. Some major libraries will hold hard copies of these types of publications. Otherwise, they might be accessible through the internet or via microfilms held by the Church of Jesus Christ of Latter-Day Saints (Mormons).

Australians can use Trove to locate libraries that hold publications of interest. Many of these publications can be obtained via inter-library loans. Trove also provides free access to Australia's online newspapers. Sometimes journalists took country trips and their newspapers published the resulting reports. The descriptions of the towns and villages and highways and byways can provide useful sources of factual and descriptive information. In fact, if you find that a journalist has taken a trip in an area that interests you, it is a good idea to print out all the reports so they are easily accessed at a later time.

It is important not to dump factual information into a family history, though. It needs to be woven through. This is discussed later in this publication and also in the companion publication.

Emigration experiences

Every person who emigrated from Europe or other parts of the world to America, Canada, Australia, New Zealand or South Africa prior to the mid-twentieth century travelled by sea.

Before I go any further, let me clarify a word usage that many family historians struggle with. The word *emigrate* relates to departure and *immigrate* to arrival, while *migrate* is non-specific. Correct usage is: 'Many Irish people *emigrated* to Australia and America after the potato famine' or 'America had many Irish *immigrants*'. For those struggling to work out which form should be used, we should try to mentally position ourselves (as the narrator) in the country we are writing about. If we have just been describing a person's life in Ireland, we the narrator are standing on Ireland's shores. If we then discuss the person's decision to begin again in another country, we are referring to their decision to *emigrate*. Once we have travelled with them to Australia or America or wherever and are standing on the shores of their new home, we can then discuss their life as an *immigrant*. If this seems completely confusing, just use *migrate* and *migrant*: less professional but at least accurate.

Most family histories record the ship-name and the date and place of departure, and the same for the ports of call and place of arrival. That's all. Yet dates of departure and arrival are only as accurate as the surviving records allow them to be. Any Australian researcher who has used J.S. Cumpston's *Shipping Arrivals and Departures, Sydney, 1788-1825* (Roebuck, 1977) will have noticed how often two dates of arrival are listed for the same ship. This is because different original sources recorded different dates, as incredible as that may seem.

Some researchers push past their own family's horizons by finding other sources to help them describe their family's voyage: the journal of a fellow passenger, the captain or surgeon's log, or a newspaper report published after the vessel's arrival. The growing availability of online newspapers can be extremely helpful in finding newspaper reports about the ship or about other people who travelled on the same ship. I recently found a letter published in a newspaper that was written by a soldier who travelled on the same ship as my protagonist to serve in World War 1.

For those researching Australians, Ian Nicholson's *Log of Logs* series (also Roebuck) provides a useful guide to many surviving journals and logs. It also notes where they are held.

If nothing useful has survived for a voyage of interest, look for the journals of those who made a similar journey. These can at least help us gain a sense of the experience.

For those researching Australian convicts, for example,

Peter Cunningham described his experiences as the surgeon superintendent of some 1820s convict transports in *Two Years in New South Wales* (Royal Australian Historical Society, 1966). This book provides fascinating insights into the convicts as a social group as well as painting a picture of New South Wales in the 1820s. Dr John Haslam travelled as Surgeon Superintendent on the convict transport *Mariner* in 1815, a naïve evangelical Christian desperate to convert the convicts in his care. His journal recounting the frustrations of dealing with his intransigent charges proved extremely funny – quite unintentionally, I'm sure.

Don't stop at gathering a general sense of the voyage. Again, think about other possibilities. If the basic information normally included in a family history – the dates – are only probabilities, what are the certainties, if any?

The realities of a voyage

During a lengthy sea voyage in the eighteenth and early nineteenth centuries, we can be certain that our ancestors and everyone else travelling by sea would have seen and heard and smelt and tasted and felt similar things. Billowing white sails. The creaking of the wooden hull. The briny smell of the ocean. The salty tang of seawater. The splash of water droplets on their skin.

While dates slide past us, sensory images wrap themselves around us. As we read these words we are immediately transported onto the deck of a ship, our ancestor's ship. We see, hear, taste, smell and feel everything our ancestor is seeing, hearing, tasting, smelling and feeling. This is the reality of their experience.

Conversely, many of our ancestors – the illiterate in particular – would never have known what date they departed their home country or what date they arrived or departed from a port of call or what date they docked in their new country. Nor would they have cared. Yet these dates are often the only details recorded in family histories. The sensory details – the certainties on a long sea voyage – are ignored as they are not 'facts'.

Well, 'facts' ain't necessarily *facts*.

Providing scenic descriptions

If we use dates merely as pathways, we can transform these dry basics into something detailed and evocative. In three of my books, I had to describe my protagonist's arrival in Sydney when the only known information was the name of his or her ship and its date of arrival. This was an important moment in their lives so I had to make it interesting. Somehow.

In my first book, I chose the easy way out. I used someone else's impressions:

> After a voyage of less than a week, the *Medway* sailed into Sydney Harbour early in October 1827. Some years later a judicial appointee reminisced about his own arrival in Sydney around that time. Sir Roger Therry described passing through the guardian giants at the entrance to Port Jackson which served as a keyhole to the magnificent harbour in front of him. He marvelled at its deep crystal waters and the broad canal dotted with islets and bounded by sandy inlets which led to the Sydney Cove settlement ...

Naturally, I couldn't use someone else's impressions a second time. In my second book, the narrator's words were my own but the perspective was from the deck of the vessel:

> The *Mariner* slipped through safely and for those fortunate enough to be on deck one of the most beautiful harbours in the world offered up its treasures.

And the third book? This time I thought seriously about bypassing the arrival altogether – until I had an idea. What is the narrator's perspective in the following description?

> A frisson of trepidation rippled through the busy harbour port of Sydney. The convict transport *Marquis Wellington* was tacking through the choppy seas separating the North and South Heads, the sentries guarding Port Jackson from the ocean's malevolence. Soon it would steer along the calm turquoise waters of the channel, around little tree-dotted islands, past

craggy bluffs and scrubby banks and romantic golden bays, and enter Sydney Cove.

It wasn't the transport's arrival that worried Sydney but what its people would discover when the hatches were unlocked and thrown back, and its cargo of crime unloaded. Sydney had greeted seven convict transports the previous year, more than double the usual number, and every second vessel had brought a tale of horror ...

The perspective, of course, is from Sydney itself as the town looks out towards the convict ship. A chapter is devoted to writing from different perspectives in *Writing and Publishing Gripping Family Histories.*

The third description also includes another quality – an undercurrent of tension – that keeps our reader intrigued. What is it that Sydney fears?

Add tension to our story and our reader is hooked. *Tension* is also discussed in the companion volume .

Drawing on our senses

Good writers draw on all of their senses when describing scenery.

Most of us automatically describe what we *see*. Here is a wonderful visual description from Ernest Hemingway who was a travel writer in a previous life:

Switzerland is a small steep country, much more up and down than sideways, and is all stuck over with large brown hotels built on the cuckoo clock style of architecture.

However, we don't only experience the world visually. Which of our senses is drawn upon in the following description written in the late 1700s by a man named David Collins?

The spot chosen was at the head of a cove, near the run of fresh water, which stole silently along through a very thick wood, the stillness of which had then, for the first time since the creation, been interrupted by the rude sound of the labourer's axe, and the downfall of its ancient inhabitants; a stillness and

> tranquillity which from that day were to give place to the voice
> of labour, the confusion of camps and towns, and the busy hum
> of its new possessors.

This evocative description is largely auditory. We *hear* the
changes in the environment wrought by British settlement rather
than *seeing* them. Sensory writing is discussed further in the
companion volume.

Descriptions that readers skip

How many times have we started reading a paragraph in a book
then stopped and jumped to the next paragraph? It is generally
because the paragraph contains nothing but description. Look at
the following prose:

> Sarah was baptised on 24 March 1799 at Deal. The church was
> built of stone and perched on the hill above the village.

The 'church' reference is an add-on sentence of description.
Imagine if that 'church' sentence was a separate and detailed
paragraph. Unless our readers have a profound interest in that
church in particular or in churches in general, many will lose
interest and skip to the next paragraph.

Description must move the story along or there is little point
in adding it because most readers will skim over it or skip it
altogether. A famous author once said that best-selling authors
are those who leave out the bits that readers skip.

Of course, literary authors like Hemingway can get away
with copious amounts of description because their words are so
poetic. The rest of us need to keep the reader engaged by making
the description part of the story. In the following sentence, the
description is embedded in the *action*.

> On 24 March 1799 Sarah's parents carried her to the little stone
> church perched on top of the hill ...

On page 92 there was a description of the *Marquis of
Wellington*'s arrival in Sydney, the one that commenced 'A

frisson of trepidation rippled through the busy harbour port...'
Imagine if that arrival description merely noted:

> ... the ship *Marquis of Wellington* reached Sydney on 27
> January 1816.
> Sydney was a busy harbour port. Ships entered Port Jackson
> through the North and South Heads and sailed for a few miles
> through the harbour before reaching Sydney Cove. Beaches
> and bays lined the harbour shores with islands in the middle.

Boring! We are beginning to skim the paragraph by the time
we reach the second line.

Adding readable descriptions

Family historians are often stuck with little more than names,
dates and places. We seek sources of description to add life to our
narrative yet there is little point in making the effort if our readers
skip over it. So how do we add description to our family histories
in a way that makes the story more interesting, that motivates our
readers to continue reading?

The three descriptions of a convict ship's arrival in Sydney
each provided a different perspective. In the latter two examples,
we, as the reader, were also a participant. We stood on the deck
looking out at the harbour, or we stood on the shore looking out at
the ship. By describing scenery this way, our readers become an
active part of the description. They are seeing the scene through
their own eyes so they are more inclined to keep reading.

The following description describes the arrival of my
protagonist, Chubbie Miller, in London:

> If she'd been asked before her holiday to imagine a word to
> describe London, it wouldn't have been 'freedom'.
> Her late father had long urged her to visit his home country.
> His England was a world of dainty whitewashed cottages
> nestling around spires that thrust resolutely towards the
> heavens, of church fetes and church dances and church picnics,
> where the vicar was loved almost as much as his god. It was a

world of moral rectitude and righteousness, of class and, most importantly, tradition. Everyone had their place and – so long as they accepted it – all was right with the world.

The lure for her had been different, touristy more than anything. Drinking tea beside the Thames as it slipped through the greatest city in the western world. Strolling across the romantic London Bridge. Ogling the Crown Jewels that shimmered with the nation's wealth and importance ...

In this description, we see London through her eyes – and those of her late father. The description doesn't *tell* the reader what it looks like. It *shows* us her perception of the city. In doing so, it communicates information about her character and her family background and also progesses the story.

Did this information come from Chubbie's own accounts? No. While her personal accounts provide a huge amount of information, I needed to go beyond them to write her story. I needed to know enough about her family background and character that I could read between the lines and communicate the essence as well as the facts of her experiences. I needed to make authorial judgements in order to bring Chubbie and her story alive for readers.

A skilled family history writer will do the same.

Character in the environment

Good description not only paints a graphic word picture, it helps communicate character. Most family historians think of humans alone as having character. When these researchers can only find names, dates and places, they decide that it is safer to ignore character altogether.

In truth, everything has a character and if we can capture the essence of anything we can add life to our narrative.

As the crew struck and furled the sails, the town loomed closer. Those on deck could see Government House on the eastern ridge, a pleasant two-storied building with columns and a verandah. It was the hub of law and order in the community, the core of power and political largesse. With symbolic symmetry, the western ridge bore the 'pepper castor' tower of St Philip's Church. While the law attempted to constrain the physical activities of the populace, the church took responsibility for the moral.

Not only are we seeing Sydney through the eyes of those on board, we are 'seeing' the social and political dynamics of the place.

What about the town's character?

The Rocks [the night-life district] had shrugged off the church's frowns, kicked off the law's chains. It was bold and saucy, determined to enjoy life on its own terms.

People and places are not alone in having character. Think about mountains, buildings, ships. Capturing a sense of character is as easy as adding a descriptive adjective to our common noun: an *imperious* clipper, a *belligerent* tug.

Summary
We cannot write interesting family histories if we just stick to the facts. We have to delve much deeper using our knowledge of human nature and also of the similarities between different events and the natural human reaction to them.

15

Epigraphs

Did you notice the stand-alone quote on an otherwise blank page at the start of this publication? It is called an *epigraph*. We can use epigraphs at the start of a section or chapter of a book. We can use them to capture the essence of a person's life, or to depict something about that person's life, or to offer our readers a foretaste of what is to come – or what is not to come, if we are being playful. And, importantly, we don't have to write anything. We just have to find appropriate descriptions written by someone else.

Good quotes are easy to find on the internet. We just type into our search engine the word 'quote' then whatever we are searching for: 'love', 'death', 'Shakespeare death', 'Charles Dickens' or a place name or occupational term. Epigraphs add so powerfully to the prose of less experienced writers that I have transformed what was a couple of pages in the first edition into an entire chapter.

The layout for a chapter epigraph is shown below. Note that we need to indent the paragraph both on the left and right. It is acceptable to have a justified or a ragged edge paragraph. The following example is centred:

Chapter 1

Jessie 'Chubbie' Miller

A woman flying an airplane is like an
elephant walking on its hind legs –
neither of them do the trick especially well,
but I'm surprised to see them doing it at all.

Cy Caldwell, *Aero Digest*, September 1929

I had intended to use the above quote to expose – to *show* rather than *tell* – the misogyny female aviators faced in the 1920s however my publisher decided that *Chubbie Miller* didn't need epigraphs because of its fast pace. So I've used the opportunity to slip it in here.

An important point to remember when we include epigraphs is to control the layout. Think of an epigraph as if it is a poem. The line breaks are as important as the words communicated. Observe the difference in dramatic effect if I had allowed the typesetting programme to control the layout of the above epigraph:

> A woman flying an airplane is like an elephant
> walking on its hind legs – neither of them do the
> trick especially well, but I'm surprised to see them
> doing it at all.

Locational

Epigraphs about places are particularly apt for family historians for the simple reason that our ancestors always lived somewhere. One of the best sources of locational epigraphs are poems. These are often included in histories of a town or village. Otherwise, google 'poem' and the name of our place of interest. The following poem about a parish in Lanarkshire, Scotland is from J. Loudon's *Our Own Town: A Short History of Shotts*.

> Know ye the land where the dark herbless whinstone
> In hillocks not hills rears its desolate head?
> Where poverty chains down the nose to the grindstone,
> Till the heart and the soul are as heavy as lead?
> Where the crops never ripen, the rose cannot blow,
> And the sunshine of summer scarce melteth the snow?
> 'Tis the parish of Shotts, a place which the sun
> Cannot bless with his beams; which he hates to shine on.

After reading this poem, I could understand why my ancestors left Shotts for the bright lights of Edinburgh.

Descriptive

The following comes from Jeremy Bentham's *The Rationale of Punishment*:

> 'I sentence you,' says the Judge, 'but to what I know not: perhaps to storm and shipwreck; perhaps to infectious diseases; perhaps to famine; perhaps to be massacred by savages; perhaps to be devoured by wild beasts. Away, take your chance; perish or prosper, suffer or enjoy; I rid myself of the sight of you; the ship that bears you away saves me from witnessing your sufferings.'

This British judge was sentencing a prisoner to transportation to America (yes, America, not Australia), yet his words communicate the essence of any transportation experience. Indeed, his words communicate a sense of the migration experience in general. The social environment of the time might have 'sentenced' our ancestors to begin again in another country, in America, Canada, Africa, Australia or New Zealand. As they embarked on their ships, they would have felt immense trepidation because they had no idea what the future would hold.

Reportedly, Ireland's biggest export industry in the 1800s was its people. This also leads us to think about the historical 'push and pull' factors in our ancestors' lives, the factors that pushed an ancestors from one country and pulled them towards another. This is an important theme in any family history that documents the story of a person who relocates from one country to another.

Criminal

Many of us world-wide, and particularly those who descend from early Australian settlers, have criminal ancestors. Great quotes from the past beg to be used. We have the generalist allusion from Sir Walter Scott:

> Oh, what a tangled web we weave,
> When first we practise to deceive!

We can offer a moral judgement, in the words of others, when we write about the laws of the past. The following convict's defence serves an indictment of the British penal system:

> If I have been bad, Your Honor,
> what has been done to make me better?

As for capital punishment, *Punch* so aptly captured its hypocrisy as long ago as the 1840s:

> We hire the hangman to preach to the world
> the sacredness of human life.

Because my first five mainstream books are about criminals, anyone who has criminal ancestry – British, Australian or other – will find dozens of appropriate epigraphs in the publications.

Occupational

The previously mentioned lines from Longfellow's *A Village Blacksmith* could be used as an epigraph for an ancestor who worked as a blacksmith, a common occupation in times gone by.

One of my ancestors had a haberdashery shop so I used this clever rhyming advertisement as an epigraph:

> Every sort of hose and socks,
> Gloves for scientific knocks;
> Braces, garters, stiffners, stocks,
> Shirts, chemises, children's frocks;
> Combs, hair-brushes, caoutchouc braces;
> Nutmeg-graters, waistcoat-springs,
> Parasol, or baby's rings;
> Packing-needles, necklace snaps,
> Bonnets, brief-bags, peaks for caps;
> Scrubbing-brushes, trowsers'-straps,
> Hundreds of other useful traps,
> Nearly all you stand of need in
> Can be well obtained of PEDEN.

Perhaps an ancestor was an early nurse. We could quote Florence Nightingale:

> It may seem a strange principle to enunciate
> as the very first requirement in a hospital
> that it should do the sick no harm.

Historical

Epigraphs can be ideal for setting the historical scene. Perhaps we are writing about someone who lived through the Great Depression. We can foreshadow the drama that followed the Wall Street Crash of 1929 by using as an epigraph William Feather's perceptive remark about stock markets:

> One of the funny things about the stock market
> is that every time one person buys, another sells,
> and both think they are astute.

If we are writing about a World War II soldier, it is hard to go past Winston Churchill's famous speech:

> We shall defend our island, whatever the cost may be,
> we shall fight on the beaches,
> we shall fight on the landing grounds,
> we shall fight in the fields and in the streets,
> we shall fight in the hills;
> we shall never surrender.

Humorous

Some epigraphs can be light-hearted, even wry, communicating to the reader that we mustn't take ourselves too seriously. The following anonymous epigraph is ideal for anyone writing the story of a convict transported to Australia.

> Of course Australia is marked for glory
> because its people have been chosen
> by the finest judges in England.

And the following is ideal for anyone writing about an aviator facing a serious airborne problem. The source is also unknown:

> The three most common expressions in aviation are:
>
> 'Where am I?',
> 'Why is it doing that?'
> and 'Oh crap!'

Character

Epigraphs can be chosen to communicate any aspect of human behaviour or character covered in our chapter. Deciding to emigrate to another country takes courage. Mark Twain aptly described this quality:

> Courage is resistance to fear, mastery of fear,
> not absence of fear.

Tongue-in-cheek is always enjoyable. It is fun to write and to think about our readers' gradual awakening – although it might take them a second reading for full appreciation. The following quote, taken from the *Tasmanian and Asiatic Review*, began a chapter in *An Irresistible Temptation* about John Stephen Jr's lying, cheating, adulterous behaviour:

> John Stephen Jnr has possessed himself of
> general esteem in New South Wales for his
> open, frank, liberal and gentlemanly conduct.

Relationships

Perhaps two of our ancestors had a rocky marriage. This quote from the master, William Shakespeare, is ideal:

> The course of true love never did run smooth.

Charles Dickens captured the problems we face in our dealings with other people in this quote:

A wonderful fact to reflect upon,
that every human creature is constituted to be that
profound secret and mystery to every other.

Perhaps our ancestor conspired to deceive someone or suffered from another's treachery. Leonardo da Vinci described treachery beautifully:

The bee may be likened to deceit
for it has honey in its mouth and poison behind.

Foreshadowing

Some epigraphs can foreshadow. We know when we read this quote from Robert Burns that something is about to go seriously wrong:

The best laid schemes o' mice an' men ...

Or from William Shakespeare:

When clouds appear, wise men put on their cloaks.

Or from Charles Dickens:

Always suspect everybody.

Your readers will be intrigued before they have even read the first word of the chapter.

Summary

Finding appropriate or tongue-in-cheek epigraphs is an enjoyable exercise in itself. Many journalists and novelists were deliciously quotable in the past – and even today. We need to train ourselves to recognise good quotes, those that would be perfect for epigraphs, and to jot them down even if we can't yet think of somewhere to put them. I came across the da Vinci quote about deceit while reading a crime thriller.

16

Words, words, words

Words are the most powerful tools at our disposal when writing a family history. Sure, we have charts and pictures and maps; nevertheless, words are the glue that holds everything together. Words are a writer's best friend. So how can we make the best use of them when we write our family histories?

The simplest English sentence contains a noun (the subject) and a verb (the 'doing' word) as we were all taught at school. Adjectives and adverbs add colour to our nouns and verbs respectively however the word that actually transmits our sentence's energy is the verb. It is critical that we think carefully about all of our verbs.

Verbs
Which of the following sentences has the most oomph?

Napoleon said loudly.

Napoleon roared.

While *said* is also a verb (and *loudly* an adverb), *said* is a 'nothing' word that slips past us without being noticed.

Went is the same. We should avoid it and all the other 'nothing words' of our day-to-day conversation and writing. Instead, we should replace it with words that communicate a true sense of movement and experience:

She went in a carriage from London to ...

Her carriage rattled and lurched along the pot-holed roads as she travelled from London to ...

In the second example, the journey becomes an actual experience for our ancestor, not just a 'beam me up Scotty' moment. And we lurch along the pot-holed roads with her.

But how can we know that her carriage *rattled and lurched* and that the roads were *pot-holed*? A bit of background reading about roads and carriage trips in the eighteenth and nineteenth centuries will answer that. We can also use our logic and imagination because everyone, surely, has driven along a dirt road. And we still have potholes in our modern roads unless they are regularly resurfaced. There can be no doubt whatsoever that our ancestors' wooden- or metal-wheeled carriages or carts would have rattled and lurched along pot-holed roads at some point during their journeys.

Let's think about trips by sea. *Sailed* is a more evocative word than *went* in reference to a sea journey. Even better are words such as *scudded, pitched, rolled*. For those who get seasick – sorry.

What about *went* in relation to a person walking from one place to another. We could instead use *trudged, beetled, stalked, sashayed*. These verbs are not only more evocative, some of them communicate character as well as movement.

But, you might ask, how can we know enough about our ancestors or the events in their lives to use such replacement words? That's when we draw upon logic and imagination. Let's start with something simple.

The *Mariner*'s convicts disembarked at daybreak.

Rowed ashore at daybreak, the *Mariner*'s convicts staggered off the boat ...

The first *Mariner* sentence is not only dry, it fails to communicate any sense of the disembarkation experience. The men had been at sea for months and were shackled so they were unlikely to step daintily ashore on legs that would instantly adjust to being on dry land. What would they do? Think about it ... visualise it ... Yes, they would stagger. So we need to give ourselves permission to use our logic and imagination and write evocatively.

Concrete images

It is important that we anchor our verbs in concrete images, where possible, using words that depict an action or experience rather than those that slip over the tops of our heads. *Went* does not provide a concrete image. We cannot see a person 'went-ing' – that is, 'going'. However we can see a carriage *rattling and lurching* and we can see a ship *scudding* and we can see people being *rowed* ashore and *staggering* off the boat.

How else can we use energetic verbs to add life to our family history, particularly when we cannot find any information that shows our ancestor actually doing anything?

England cowered under the threat of a French invasion.

England basked in the glory of the Waterloo victory.

Each of these sentences relies upon its verb for its energy– that is, *cower* or *bask*. But there's more. We could say 'Britain feared a French invasion' – *feared* being the verb – however this sentence has little energy, no oomph at all. Why? Because it doesn't create a visual image. While we can see someone 'cowering with fear', we cannot see someone 'fearing'.

Each of these sentences uses the writing technique known as personification – that is, attributing human characteristics to inanimate objects or abstract ideas. Instead of making up what one person, our ancestor, is thinking or feeling or doing, we can use personification to indirectly reflect it. Britain is not an entity that can cower or bask, but its people can and that's what these words are communicating. Britain's people, of course, include our ancestors.

Nouns

Be as specific as possible when choosing nouns. Burrow down until the exact word pops up. For example, a word like *boat* generates only a fuzzy image in our readers' minds because there are so many different types of boats. There are large and small boats, passenger liners, tugs, barges, row-boats. If our ancestor travelled somewhere by boat, try to identify what type it was and use the specific word. The image created in our minds when we hear *boat* and *clipper* is quite different.

Think of the word *bird*. If we were asked to describe the image our brain conjures up when we hear the word 'bird', the image described by each of us would be different. However, if we were asked to describe our images for the word *seagull*, the images would be almost identical. We don't need to use a wordy description – 'grey and white, found near the water, likes stealing food from people' – to communicate the appropriate image.

Adjectives and adverbs

Beginner writers often add adjectives and adverbs into their writing willy-nilly. It is wise to cut out any that aren't necessary. If we have a string of adjectives, try to cut four to three, three to two, and so on. Retain adjectives and adverbs only if they are truly descriptive or are original.

For example, instead of a *noisy bird*, it might be more appropriate to write a *squabbling seagull*.

And, as mentioned at the top of this chapter, try to replace a verb-adverb combination with a stronger verb.

> He said with annoyance …

> He grumbled …

Or:

> The carriage moved quickly along the road …

> The carriage hurtled along the road …

I have built up a word bank file, a huge thesaurus, for some words I regularly use in my writing. One section includes words for physical movements. Some are listed below:

> Amble, beetle, bound, bustle, canter, career, charge, clomp, clump, crawl, creep, dart, dash, dawdle, dodder, drive, flit, flee, float, flop, flounce, flounder, fly, gallop, gambol, glide, hasten.

Metaphors and similes

Metaphors and similes are other tools we can use. Both are figures of speech that liken one thing to another in a way that creates a picture or sensory experience for the reader.

Metaphors are phrases or sentences that describe something as if it *is* something else. At the start of this chapter I wrote 'words are the glue that holds everything together'. That's a metaphor. Here is a stunning metaphor written by Gay Talese:

> Sinatra with a cold is Picasso without paint,
> Ferrari without fuel – only worse.

Or this one (author unknown):

> His ambitions were
> shipwrecked on the reefs of scandal.

Similes are phrases or sentences that describe something as if it is *similar to* something else, using the words *as* or *like*. Here are two *like* examples:

> Like a deadly snake it was difficult to control and,
> when released, discharged its fury
> in one explosive surge.

> The escort planes buzzed around like angry hornets.

And here are two *as* examples:

> … singing voices as rich as clotted cream …

> The pilots' bane greeted them, the thick gauze-
> like shroud that enveloped everything as if a giant
> eraser had swooped in overnight and obliterated
> their surroundings.

For some writers, similes and metaphors instantly spring to mind; they tend to be visual people. Others have greater difficulty in crafting a suitable simile or metaphor. If these are proving difficult to craft, forget about using them. Better to have no similes and metaphors than ones that confuse our readers or, even worse, make them cringe.

Active versus passive voice

When I used to read my daughter's university essays, I often pointed out that she was using the passive voice whereas the active voice would be more effective (in fact, I reminded her so often that I would see her hackles rise as soon as I mentioned the phrase.) No doubt many other Word users who see the squiggly green line under their sentence and the explanation 'passive voice' probably don't understand the concept as well. So I am going to make it obvious by quoting a comic piece from a book about writing humour.

One strategy for writing humour relies upon taking something to its extreme, to the point at which it becomes totally absurd. Comedian John Vordaus in his book *The Comic Toolbox* writes that he had been taught by the experts to religiously purge the passive voice from his writing until one day he couldn't control the urge any longer:

> The room was walked into by a man by whom strong, handsome features were had. A woman was met by him. The bed was laid upon by her. Then the bed was lain upon by him. Clothing was removed from them both. Sex was had. Afterwards, cigarettes were smoked by them. Suddenly the door was opened by the husband of the woman by whom the bed was lain upon. A gun was held by him ...

Every sentence is written in the passive voice. The active voice would of course say:

> The strong handsome man walked into the room ...

If we eradicate unnecessary passive sentences from our writing and replace weak verbs with strong verbs, we will instantly add life to our narrative.

Start by looking for the word *was*. It indicates a weak verb; for example, *was going*, which is another version of *went*. Having found the word *was*, see if it also indicates a passive sentence structure. Do so by mentally swapping the parts of the sentence around.

She was baptised ...

This is a passive sentence because we haven't allowed the doer to do the doing. The active version is:

The clergyman baptised her ...

If the subject of the sentence, the person who does whatever is being done, does not appear at the start of the sentence then it is a passive sentence. Once we get used to identifying passive sentences of this nature, we will find it easier to recognise all passive sentences.

Sometimes we intend to write a passive sentence:

She was buried four days later ...

The active version is, of course, 'He/She/They buried her four days later ...' However, if we are not interested in the 'he/she/they' but only in the person being buried, then our sentence structure conveys the meaning we intend.

If we locate a passive sentence, we should make sure that we really do require such a sentence structure to best communicate our meaning. If not, we should try to transform it into an active sentence. University students are generally trained to write passive sentences so it requires a major re-adjustment to eradicate these from their writing. (Note that this sentence is in the passive voice. Why? I neither wanted nor needed to draw attention to the university lecturers who taught them, which would have been the result if I had commenced the sentence, 'University lecturers generally train students to write passive sentences ...')

A point worth remembering is that, even though a student might receive good marks for a university essay, the style that generated the good marks will not necessarily work in the broader market. In fact, few academics get contracts to write for the commercial market because the writing styles are so different. Even the output of university courses that teach creative writing are not necessarily suitable for the mainstream market. I once heard that novels that are written as part of creative writing Master degrees and PhDs are rarely picked up by mainstream publishers.

Summary

I could write an entire book about writing techniques; however, as many others have already done so, let's be guided by their wisdom. A list of worthwhile writing books is found in the Reading List at the end of this publication and a different list at the end of *Writing and Publishing Gripping Family Histories*. I regularly re-read them to refresh my mind and something new resonates with me each time, helping to develop my own writing skills.

I cannot stress too strongly that the more we learn, the easier it gets. We all read books and articles about tracing our ancestors to help increase our research skills. In the same way, anyone planning to write a family history – that is, everyone reading this book – should read books about writing. If money is limited, start with *Words Fail Me*. It is light, funny and extremely helpful.

17

Delight in the unexpected

The 'biographies' I recommend writing generally tell the story of two people: a husband and a wife. Sometimes they discuss only one person, usually the woman, because our ancestor was born out of wedlock and its father's details were not documented. Occasionally, only the man's name is known because the baby's baptism entry – filled out, no doubt, by a man – failed to recognise the mother's crucial role in carrying the baby for that extremely long nine-month gestational period then enduring the unavoidable and painful birth.

Even if the woman's name is known, additional information can be difficult to find. Prior to Britain's Married Women's Property Rights Act of 1882, for example, a woman surrendered her property to her husband upon marriage. As a result, many of our female ancestors are almost invisible from an archival perspective. They are mentioned on the occasional page in a church or civil register, but that's all. Yet sometimes their voices call from between the lines so it is important to be listening.

Read between the lines

When writing one family history, I was given a copy of a diary written by a family member. The diary mentioned, in an intrigued tone, a baby left on the doorstep of the man's brother's house. Thereafter the topic was ignored altogether. Being curious – and suspicious – I started searching the newspapers. I soon discovered the truth: the brother had strayed.

Prior to that time, the brother and his wife had produced children every two years and I had noticed and wondered about the five-year gap before their next child was born. Suddenly I had an explanation.

That gap weeps of the wife's heartache and anger.

Some women, who had no voice in life, found it in death. In 1788, Anne Willis used her will to tell the world of her husband's cruelty:

> ... my life has been that of perfect slavery and misery and though the principal foundation of my ailments proceeded from his inhumanity and neglect he never let me feel one indulgence. The only enjoyment I coveted or my health would suffer me to feel was the society of my sister and two brothers but he found that too great a comfort and soon by a rudeness of behavior which he constantly studied and treated them with in his own house, rendered the house to them hateful and distressed my heart and mind to wretchedness ...

Research the spouse's background

Many genealogists don't bother researching the other partner, that is, the husband or wife they are not descended from, particularly if that spouse bore no children with their ancestor. Anne Willis was the second wife so, for these genealogists, her voice was muzzled by her childlessness.

Don't ignore the other spouse. They were an important part of our ancestor's life and for that reason alone they should have their story told. And what fascinating and disturbing insights would have been missed if this second Willis wife had not been researched.

Many family historians who write broom-shaped or pyramid-shaped family histories – that is, they explore the lives of multiple family members in a single generational line – include barely any information about the partner of their non-ancestral couples. They slip this man or woman into the family history as if he or she came into existence on the marriage day, or was born, went into limbo-land for a couple of decades, then resurfaced just in time to be married. It is important to remember that all of us bring into our marriages the experiences of our childhoods and family backgrounds and that the same was true in previous generations. Try to explore the spouses' family backgrounds as much as possible. The most interesting stories in our family histories might originate with the spouse's family.

If I hadn't researched the family background of the spouses in my Nash family history – my ancestor's cousin's husband's parents, to be precise – I would never have found the story of the Jane New scandal or tried writing popular history. Nor would this book have been written.

Don't cut corners

While researching *Breaking the Bank*, I discovered that three of my protagonists were incarcerated on a prison hulk prior to being transported to a secondary penal settlement, so I started searching hulk records. Three different microfilms included weekly registers for the hulk. I found the first, opened the box, wound on the microfilm, looked at page after page until I found the first protagonist, then continued looking for the second, then the third. I found that two of the men were dispatched to the transport on the same day and the third two months later. There was no explanation for the later departure. I wondered if the man was ill and deemed unfit to make the journey.

I wound the microfilm off and put the reel back in its box and on the shelf then followed the same process with the next reel. It contained exactly the same information as the first microfilm. I went through the same process for the third microfilm and found the first entry, which contained exactly the same information as the previous two microfilms. This process had taken a considerable amount of time and for a moment – a split second – I considered abandoning the search for the other two bank robbers. But I resisted the urge. Fortunately. On this third reel, against the entry for the man transported two months later, was one additional word: 'ran'.

There was my interesting story. It turned out that he and his companions had filed off their ankle irons as well as the iron bars on their porthole, stripped off their clothes, squeezed through the porthole, dropped down into the sewerage-strewn muck surrounding the hulk and swum towards the shore as shots were fired into the water around them.

Those who cut corners never know what they have missed.

Explore the unusual

Tattoos over half the body of a female ancestor? The outer half.

The same friend who discovered the Kings and Queens in her family history had stepped onto that ancestral pathway when she began tracing her female end-of-the-surname-line ancestor, Blanche Irene Kane. Blanche was the daughter of a drunken and impecunious solicitor whose well-bred English family was no doubt relieved when he skedaddled to the colonies in 1870. A few years after the Kanes' arrival in Melbourne, Blanche's mother died and her father effectively abandoned his children. Blanche was caught soliciting in Carlton Gardens at the age of fourteen – 'a very bad girl', claimed the police report. 'A very bad father' is no doubt a more accurate description.

As my friend continued researching she discovered four unregistered children of unknown paternity, a marriage to a 'Chinaman' and, later in Blanche's tough life, incarceration in an institution. The institution's paperwork mentioned the tattoos.

Sometimes the answers to questions can never be found – for instance, why Blanche chose to be tattooed – but that doesn't prevent us from speculating. Explore the unusual, anything that will make our family history interesting. In this case, rather than obsessing with the dates of her incarceration, it is much more interesting to research tattoos. How many women had tattoos at that time, what type of women were they (we can probably guess), what type of tattoos and how was it done? This is fascinating stuff. But again don't focus on the facts. Try to bring this information to life by evoking sensory images.

18

The truth, the whole truth ...

I am sure many people have come across the following amusing anecdote:

> A wealthy family commissioned an author to write its history but stipulated that he'd have to find some way of softening the fact that one member had ended a life of crime by being electrocuted in the electric chair. They were delighted with the results. "Uncle William occupied a chair of applied electronics in a leading government institution. He was held to the post by the closest of ties and his death came as a real shock."

It is probably a genealogical myth although it is clever nonetheless. But, seriously, what does this tell us about such a family history. Hagiography, at the very least, and of questionable accuracy by any definition. What else were they hiding?

Which begs an answer to the question: how far can we go, indeed how far must we go, in telling the truth in our family histories?

The first point to remember is that we are writing history not fiction. If people don't want to know anything 'bad' about their ancestors, they shouldn't trace their family history because, inevitably, someone will have broken a law or social moré, either of their own time or of ours. That being said, there are a couple of issues that need careful treatment, so let's deal with those first.

Unknown adoptions

What if we discover that someone who is still living was adopted and doesn't know about it?

If we are writing a family history just for our immediate family, then we should rely on our own judgement. However, if we are writing a pyramid- or broom-shaped family history and gathering little bits of information about a lot of people, this could be a problem. What would be my suggestion?

Don't!

Writing about living people is dangerous. Family secrets tend to come out at the worst possible time for the parties involved and the revelation, unwitting or otherwise, might come back to haunt us as well. Indeed, we could be sued.

Moreover, pyramid-shaped or broom-shaped family histories that come down to the present day are rarely interesting. They tend to comprise little more than names and dates for endless numbers of people: 'John Smith was born on 26 March 1956 and works as a baker. He married Mary Jane Clarke, a secretary, on 18 December 1980. They have two children ...' and so on, person after person after endless person.

Few people actually read such family histories. They might buy a copy, glance at the details for their own family, start reading some of the other bits but quickly become bored and put the book aside for another day (which never comes). All our hard work ends up sitting on their shelves gathering dust.

One solution is to document families for a certain number of generations, then include a chart at the back of the book so descendants can include details of their own descent from the people mentioned in the preceding biographies. Problem solved.

Rape

What if we discover that a woman was raped, a woman who was known by some members of the family (perhaps a grandmother or great-grandmother), with a branch of the family descending from a child conceived from that rape?

I can only offer my opinion. A woman who has been raped has suffered enough. Don't rape her memory. If she kept this information secret then respect her memory and keep it secret. If someone needs to know for medical reasons (or whatever) then tell them privately. But let her life mean more than just being the victim of a vicious assault.

If the rape occurred a long time ago, a couple of hundred years maybe, then it shouldn't damage a descendant's sense of themselves, so it probably isn't an issue. However, it might be worth discussing the situation with members of that branch of the family before publishing the information.

Illegitimacy

It always amuses me that some people can accept an ancestor's criminality more readily than their illegitimacy. When I was project officer for the Australian Biographical and Genealogical Record, contributors filled in forms with details about their ancestors. One part of the form asked contributors if their ancestors were married, then provided spaces to fill in the dates and places and so on. One lady had a number of early colonial ancestors, convicts among them, and on each form she wrote over the whole marriage section in huge letters:

YES!!!

But she didn't provide the date or details of marriage because her ancestors were not married. This lady could accept that her ancestors had breached society's legal code but not her own moral code. Imagine what her family histories would be like.

It is worth remembering that all of us descend from illegitimate parents somewhere in our ancestry (it wasn't the children who did anything 'wrong'). As for the other common prejudices: Protestants with British roots have centuries of Catholics in their ancestral pool, and perhaps even some Jewish or Muslim ancestry – if the family's roots lay further east. Tracing our family history necessitates accepting our past, whatever it may contain. And perhaps by learning about who we are and where we came from, we will realise that under the skin we are all the same.

But enough philosophising. How do we deal with the fact that great-aunt Maud might be deeply upset to learn that her mother was illegitimate?

First of all, many family historians have discovered that those who are particularly prudish often have their own secrets to hide, so great-aunt Maud might not be as shocked as we think. She might even know the truth about her mother's illegitimacy.

However, one way to deal with the problem is to broach the subject gently and give her time to adjust to the information before the book comes out and everyone knows about it. Remind her that no one born after the Second World War will think twice about it, nor judge her or her mother in any way (those who react in such a way are generally most worried about 'what the neighbours will think').

Or we can take the opposite path (reverse psychology) and warn her that there is something absolutely dreadful that we've discovered in our research, some information that will truly shock her so she would be well-advised not to read the book. This will produce one of two reactions. Either she will decide not to read the book, in which case we don't need to worry about upsetting her. Or she will be so curious (human nature) that she will grab a copy. When she discovers that the only 'bad' thing was that her mother was born out of wedlock, she will think 'is that all?' because by then she would have thought of much worse scenarios – for example, that an ancestor was a rapist or a murderer. Let's be frank: how bad is illegitimacy? In the real scheme of things, the only difference between a 'legitimate' child and an 'illegitimate' child is a piece of paper.

Along the same lines, it is helpful to add a bold warning notice on our family history flyer advising that our book includes tales of crime and illicit sex and that we won't take responsibility if anyone chooses to read it and is offended. The publication will fly out the door. While many family historians want perfect ancestors, publishers and advertisers learnt long ago that illicit sex and crime sell books. And our family histories are often full of them.

19

Publish or perish?

When we write family histories, we are usually doing so because we would like to publish the results of our research.

The odds of a commercial publishing company being interested in a family history, though, are so slim that it is not worth pursuing the idea. A friend of a friend wrote a book about a King of England, a book that exposed numerous fallacies in his accepted life story, but no publisher picked it up. Great book, they said, but no market. A king of England!

So don't despair. It is not necessarily a reflection on our skills, merely on what publishing companies think will sell in large enough quantities to make them money.

Self-publishing is a better option for many publications, family histories among them. Small print-run, niche market: we have total control over our publication and the profit ratio should be higher as well.

I discuss publishing in more detail in the companion volume *Writing and Publishing Gripping Family Histories*.

No single book will cover everything we want to know about writing and publishing our family histories and what slips past us in one book might resonate when we read it in another. Start by borrowing books then buy anything that seems really helpful because we are likely to return to it over and over again.

Books on self-publishing are stacked on the library bookshelves – mostly self-published, of course, and some are truly shoddy publications. Others, however, are excellent.

Knowledge is power. Gain it and use it.

Conclusion

A conclusion? I can hear the groans. How do we 'conclude' a family history?

Ending a family history without a conclusion leaves it dangling and leaves the reader feeling as if the brakes were slammed on and then there was ... nothing. An ending is important as it gives the reader a sense of completion, of closure.

Picking the right sort of conclusion is essential. We should forget the mawkishly sentimental – please. Better to hit the brakes and have our readers suffering whiplash than leave them feeling nauseated.

So what can we write in our conclusion? I previously referred to my Watson ancestor who fought for the British in the American War of Independence and whose grandson emigrated to Australia. While this family was inconsequential in the big scheme of things, their personal stories reflected world history. The conclusion is an opportunity to dwell on the fact that individuals make history, that while our lives might seem inconsequential, they are part of the bigger picture, and that it is only when we push through the fog of the present to the clear skies of the past that an individual's place in history becomes obvious.

Popular history publications often provide conclusions that look beyond the immediate to the bigger picture. Kate Colquhoun finished *Mr Briggs' Hat* with the following:

> Though no further killing would occur on a British train until 27 June 1881, the bludgeoning of Thomas Briggs in his first-class train compartment appeared symptomatic of a world spinning out of control. It seemed to prove the ability of the

disenchanted individual to wreak havoc on the national sense of security and to signify the danger was random. The fact that the attack occurred on a railway train emphasised a terrifying new reality: that technological cleverness had spawned progress and wealth, but at a cost. It suggested that the price to be paid for modernity was, even for the most privileged in society, vulnerability and death.

Whatever our ancestors did, we can be certain that their stories reflect their times – to some extent at least. So think about our ancestors' lives and how their stories might reflect history, perhaps through a 'modern' occupation or by being among the first to venture to a new area.

Here are two ideas that might be helpful in constructing a conclusion. Is it possible to bring the story full circle so that something from the introduction or the early part of the story can be returned to in the conclusion? Or is there perhaps a neat linear progression – a theme – that carries the story from the beginning to the end?

Take *An Irresistible Temptation*, for example. Researching and writing the Nash family history not only gave me the story, it gave me the ending. I discovered the story of the Jane New scandal while researching a man called Amos Crisp whose son married my ancestor's cousin. Amos's involvement in the scandal was that he hid Jane New and her lover, John Stephen Jr, when they were on the run from the authorities. As I researched Jane's story, I discovered an ironic parallel between her final escape from her pursuers (she fled from Australia to New Zealand dressed in male attire) and Amos Crisp's strategy for breaking out of gaol and, ultimately, out of the country (he slipped out of gaol dressed in female clothing). It was a parallel that someone researching Jane New's story on its own wouldn't have found. While it didn't return us to the story's beginning, it took us back to the dramatic middle. And it produced the perfect ending for the book.

Our gut will tell us when we've found the right ending.

Concluding the conclusion

On a final note, if we wish to achieve or even excel in any creative field it is worth remembering this: a survey determined that the difference between a prima ballerina (the lead soloist) and a member of the corps de ballet (the backing dancers) is 10,000 hours versus 7,000 hours. The same proved true of musicians, artists, sports-people and others who reached the top of their professions. This discovery is now called the 10,000-Hour Rule. This means that excellence is learnable – with time and effort.

Of course, to become a member of the corps de ballet, a dancer requires certain fundamentals: an appropriate physique as well as the obvious ability to dance.

What does a writer require? It's surprisingly simple: to be able to construct a sentence, then to put one sentence after another. We acquire these skills by the age of two or three. And like everything else, our abilities are honed by practice, by time and effort. Adults don't talk or write like two-year olds. Mostly.

Everyone who reads this book clearly has an interest in writing a family history. The first step in any endeavour is simply to begin.

Enjoy the journey.

Reading List

Surnames

Matthews, C.M. *How Surnames Began* (republished by Lutterworth, 2007)

Reaney, P.H. *A Dictionary of British Surnames* (republished by Oxford University Press, 2005)

Titford, John *The Penguin Dictionary of British Surnames* (Penguin, 2009)

Writing

Hall, Rayne *Writing Vivid Descriptions* [Kindle ebook]

McClanahan, Rebecca *Word Painting: A Guide to Writing More Descriptively*, Writer's Digest Book, Cincinnati, 1999

O'Conner, Patricia *Words Fail Me: What everyone who writes should know about writing*, Harcourt, San Diego, 1999

Ross-Larson, Bruce *Powerful Paragraphs*, W.W. Norton & Co., New York, 1999

Ross-Larson, *Stunning Sentences*, W.W. Norton & Co., New York, 1999

History writing

Curthoys, Ann & McGrath, Ann *How to write history that people want to read*, University of New South Wales Press, 2009

Edwards, Hazel *Writing a Non-Boring Family History*, Hale & Iremonger, Sydney, 1997

Kyle Noeline, *Writing Family History Made Very Easy: A beginner's guide*, Allen & Unwin, Sydney, 2007

Index

active history 71-2
active voice.................... 110-11
adjectives........................... 108
adoptions 117-8
adverbs 108
annotated timeline.............64-6
authorial judgements..........83-5
bibliography.................... 45, 62
broom-shaped structure......... 36
calendars......................... 14-19
character 96-7, 103
chart 38
child 73-4
conclusions 44, 122-4
criminals 100-1
death causes 75-7
dialogue 81-3
dog's dinner 37
drama 78-81
emotion.............................. 85
encyclopaedia style 29-30
endnotes.............. 44, 60-1, 62-3
epigraphs 98-104
errors 21-2
exhaustive research 115-6
faction 29
footnotes............................60-1
foreshadowing..................... 104
forgetfulness 21
given names 72-3
historical backdrop...52-3, 54-6,
70-1, 74-5, 100, 102
hooks 55
hourglass-shaped................... 37
humour 102
illegitimacy 119-20
illiteracy............................... 20
imagination 12
index 45
introductions 40-1, 51-57

journey of discovery 30-32
Lady Day 17-18
locational backdrop......71, 88-9,
92-3, 94-5, 96-7, 99
metaphors 109
migration 89-91
motivations 27
narrative non-fiction............. 33
nouns 107-8
novels 30
occupations 48-9, 73, 101
parents 73-4
passive history 71-2
passive voice.................. 110-11
perspective.................25-6, 95-6
pocket biographies 42
pole-shaped structure 36
pyramid-shaped structure ...36-7
publish 121-2
rape 118-9
relationships...................... 103-4
senses 93-4
show don't tell 85
similes 109
sources 44, 59-63, 64
spouse 114
stream of consciousness 85-7
structuring family histories35-46
surnames.................47-50, 53-4
thematic structure..............68-9
timeline..............................64-6
title 40
tone 34
tuberculosis........................76-7
unusual 116
v-shaped structure................ 37
verbs 105-8
voice 33
voyages.............................. 91

Writing and Publishing

GRIPPING

Family Histories

'Fact-driven and tedious' is how the publishing world judges the entire genre of family history writing.

Yet family histories don't need to be boring.

Carol Baxter has proven with her internationally-acclaimed, award-winning popular histories that history can be 'as lively and readable as a crime novel' (*The Times*, London). She began the journey of showing genealogists how to transform dry facts into interesting narrative in *Writing Interesting Family Histories*. She goes one step further in the long-awaited companion volume, *Writing and Publishing Gripping Family Histories*.

Visualising facts, telling stories, creating tension, enveloping readers in sensory experiences, and using story boxes to add life to drier narratives are among the topics covered in this publication. It also provides editorial tips, information about publishing options, and self-publishing guidelines.

There is no longer any reason – or excuse – for writing 'fact-driven and tedious' family histories. This book shows you how to write the opposite: gripping family histories.

www.carolbaxter.com

HELP!

Historical and Genealogical Truth:

How do I separate fact from fiction?

We sit at our computer searching for information about our ancestors and … click … we find something new and intriguing. But wait: it contradicts something else we've found. Clearly, both pieces of information can't be true. So which is true and which isn't? Or are both untrue? HELP!

Most family historians are more adept at gathering information than determining if it is accurate. An error can prove disastrous, gobbling up our precious time and money as we search in the wrong place – or worse, as we pursue the wrong ancestral line. So how do we ensure that our conclusions are accurate?

Help! Historical and Genealogical Truth: How do I separate fact from fiction? is a 'must-read' for family history detectives wishing to accurately trace their ancestry. Written in Carol Baxter's easy-to-read style, it explains how to evaluate our ancestral information so as to determine which is reliable and which is like a virus that corrupts our efforts. After reading this book, you too will be able to separate fact from fiction, truth from mistruth. Your ancestors will thank you!

www.carolbaxter.com

HELP!

Why can't I find my ancestor's surname?

How often have you sat looking at a historical register or in front of a computer screen expecting to see your ancestor's surname only to discover that it's not there? You check every spelling you can think of without success then give up the search unaware that the entry is there but that you lack enough knowledge about English letters and sounds to find it.

Help! Why can't I find my ancestor's surname? is the solution to your problem. It describes the distortions that can occur between the time your ancestor thinks about saying his or her surname to the time you search for the surname in an online index. It explains that these distortions are rarely random and displays sound charts and surnames tables showing how and why they occur. It includes lists of spellings for every letter and sound—as many as two dozen for a single vowel sound in some instances. And it provides guidelines you can follow to help find those elusive surnames.

This book is a gateway to a new world. Once you have read it, you will think about surnames in a completely different way. No longer will you be flailing in the dark, making stabs at spelling possibilities. When you follow its instructions, you will find that some of those previously abandoned surname searches are now successful.

www.carolbaxter.com

Carol Baxter's popular histories

Chubbie Miller: The Australian aviator and adventurer who beguiled the world. Set during the Golden Age of Aviation (1927-1932) it tells the story of a feisty Australian woman who become one of America's top female aviators. It is a story of adventure, drama, mystery and tragedy.

Black Widow: the true story of Australia's first female serial killer. Set in 1888/89, it tells the story of Australia's first female serial killer and is set against the backdrop of women's rights and capital punishment.

The Peculiar Case of the Electric Constable: a true tale of passion, poison and pursuit. The electric telegraph was the first commercial use of electricity. The technology was struggling commercially until New Year's Day 1845 when it was used to apprehend a murder suspect, the protagonist of this story. The consequences kick-started the Communication Revolution.

Captain Thunderbolt and His Lady: the true story of bushrangers Frederick Ward and Mary Ann Bugg. Set in the 1860s, it tells the story of Australia's 'gentleman bushranger', who was on the run from the police for nearly seven years, and his part-Aboriginal lover. It is set against the backdrop of a 'people versus the establishment' period of political and social dissent.

Breaking the Bank: An Extraordinary Colonial Robber. Set in 1828, it tells the story of Australia's largest ever bank robbery. Convicts in the penal settlement tunnelled through a sewerage drain and into the vault of the 'gentlemen's bank' stealing the equivalent, in today's terms, of about $20 million. It is set against the backdrop of the upstairs/downstairs politics of New South Wales.

An Irresistible Temptation. Set between 1829 and 1834, it tells the story of a sex scandal that rocked New South Wales and contributed to Britain's decision to recall the governor. It is set against the backdrop of the progressive versus conservative attitudes in a society that was struggling to throw off its penal settlement shackles.

www.ingramcontent.com/pod-product-compliance
Lightning Source LLC
Chambersburg PA
CBHW060631290526
45793CB00001B/217